the psychology of money

— What is the Connection between money and happiness?

ED MERID

The Psychology of Money
What is the Connection Between Money and Happiness?

By: Ed Merid

Table of Contents

Introduction

In the shadowy recesses of a bustling coffee shop, a barista's trembling hands fumble with crisp dollar bills. Her eyes, weary yet hopeful, dart between the cash register and a crumpled lottery ticket tucked in her apron. Across the room, a Wall Street mogul absent-mindedly stirs his $7 latte, his Rolex glinting under fluorescent lights as he ponders his next high-stakes deal. Two worlds, separated by zeroes on a bank statement, yet inexorably linked by an age-old question: Can money truly buy happiness?

This enigmatic relationship between wealth and well-being has perplexed philosophers, economists, and daydreamers for millennia. It's a riddle wrapped in a paradox, served with a side of cognitive dissonance. We chase the almighty dollar, euro, or yen with relentless fervor, convinced it holds the key to our happiness. Yet, how often do we pause to question this assumption?

"The Psychology of Money: What is the Connection Between Money and Happiness?" dives headfirst into this labyrinthine query. It's not merely a book; it's an expedition into the human psyche, a journey through the twisting corridors of our financial fears and fantasies. We'll scale the dizzying heights of sudden windfalls and plumb the depths of crushing debt, all in pursuit of understanding how these monetary extremes shape our emotional landscape.

But beware, dear reader. This is no dry academic tome, nor is it a get-rich-quick manual promising instant bliss through seven easy steps. Instead, prepare yourself for a rollicking adventure through neuroscience labs and Wall Street trading floors, from the ascetic monasteries of Tibet to the glittering casinos of Las Vegas. We'll dissect the brain of a lottery winner, peek into the soul of a minimalist monk, and maybe – just maybe – uncover some universal truths about what truly makes us happy.

So, fasten your seatbelts and secure your wallet. Whether you're a penny-pinching pauper or a gold-hoarding dragon, this book promises to challenge your preconceptions, tickle your neurons, and perhaps even change your relationship with money forever. After all, in a world where cash is king, isn't it time we questioned the monarchy?

Chapter 1: Challenging the Money Promised Land

Money talks, or so they say. But what if it's been feeding us a line all along?

From glossy magazines to slick TV commercials, we're bombarded with images of beaming faces aboard luxury yachts and sleek sports cars. The message? Wealth equals happiness. It's a seductive promise, as alluring as the siren's call, and potentially just as dangerous.

Let's pull back the velvet curtain on this grand illusion. We'll start by examining the ubiquitous wealth worship that permeates our society. It's not just about keeping up with the Joneses anymore; it's about surpassing them, leaving them in your gold-plated dust.

But here's where things get interesting. What if the equation we've all been sold - more money equals more joy - is fundamentally flawed? Brace yourself for a deep dive into eye-opening studies that challenge this long-held belief. We'll explore the fascinating concept of the "happiness plateau," where additional zeroes in your bank account fail to move the needle on your emotional well-being.

As we navigate this terrain, we'll encounter some surprising twists. Picture a lottery winner, euphoric at the moment, only to find themselves back at their emotional baseline mere months later. Or consider the stressed-out CEO, whose bulging wallet can't buy a good night's sleep.

Throughout this chapter, we'll peel back layers of societal conditioning and marketing manipulation. We'll question why we're so quick to equate material wealth with life satisfaction, and examine the psychological toll of this persistent pursuit.

By the time we're through, you might find yourself looking at your paycheck- or your wish list, in a whole new light. The promised land of money-fueled bliss might not be the paradise we've been led to believe. But fear not, this realization isn't a dead end, but rather the first step on a journey towards a more nuanced understanding of wealth, happiness, and the complex interplay between the two.

So, are you ready to challenge everything you thought you knew about money and happiness? Buckle up, it's going to be an illuminating ride.

1.1: The Ubiquitous Wealth Worship

In the heart of New York City, a sea of suits surges towards gleaming skyscrapers. Among them, Sarah, a fresh-faced college graduate, clutches her newly minted finance degree. Her eyes sparkle with visions of corner offices and seven-figure bonuses. This scene, replicated in financial districts worldwide, exemplifies our society's pervasive wealth worship.

But how did we get here? Let's rewind the clock.
The roots of our money mania run deep, intertwining with the very fabric of modern civilization. From the mercantile empires of old to today's tech titans, the accumulation of wealth has long been equated with success, power, and happiness. This association has been reinforced through generations, becoming as ingrained in our collective psyche as the need for food or shelter.

Take, for instance, the meteoric rise of social media influencers. These modern-day Money Muses flaunt lavish lifestyles, designer labels, and exotic locales to millions of followers. Their message? You too, can have all this , if only you had more money. It's a siren song that's hard to resist, especially for the young and ambitious.

Yet, this wealth worship isn't confined to the realms of high finance or social media. It permeates our everyday lives in subtle, insidious ways. Consider the language we use: "Time is money," "Put your money where your mouth is," "Money talks." These phrases reflect and reinforce our society's values, placing financial success on a pedestal above all else.

The media, too, plays a crucial role in perpetuating this wealth-centric worldview. News outlets breathlessly report on the latest billionaire space race or cryptocurrency boom, while glossy magazines showcase the homes of the rich and famous. Even our entertainment is saturated with money worship – from rags-to-riches stories to shows glorifying the lifestyles of the wealthy.

But here's where things get interesting. Despite this ubiquitous wealth worship, studies show that beyond a certain point, more money doesn't significantly increase happiness. Dr. Daniel Kahneman and Angus Deaton's research suggests that emotional well-being plateaus around $75,000 annual income in the US. Yet, the pursuit of wealth often continues well beyond this point.

So why do we continue to worship at the altar of affluence? The answer lies in the complex interplay of societal expectations, personal aspirations, and psychological factors. We're not just chasing money for money's sake, but for what we believe it represents: security, freedom, status, and ultimately, happiness.

As we navigate this wealth-obsessed world, it's crucial to question our assumptions and examine our motivations. Are we pursuing financial success because it aligns with our values and goals, or simply because society tells us we should?

To help you reflect on your own relationship with wealth worship, try this exercise:

1. List five things you believe money can buy that would make you happier.
2. Now, for each item, ask yourself: Is it the item itself that would bring happiness, or what it represents?
3. Finally, brainstorm alternative ways to achieve the underlying desire without spending money.

This simple exercise can be a first step in untangling the complex web of emotions and beliefs surrounding money and happiness.

As we move forward, we'll delve deeper into the psychological mechanisms behind wealth worship and explore its impact on our well-being. Remember, questioning societal norms isn't about rejecting financial success outright, but rather about cultivating a more nuanced, balanced perspective on the role of money in our lives.

1.2: Evidence That Disproves the Equation

Meet Jack, a high-powered corporate lawyer who just made partner at his prestigious firm. His annual salary has skyrocketed to seven figures, yet he finds himself staring at the ceiling each night, wondering why he feels so empty. Jack's story isn't unique. It's a living, breathing example of the growing body of evidence that challenges the long-held belief: more money equals more happiness.

Let's dive into the research that's turning this equation on its head.

First up is the groundbreaking work of psychologists Daniel Kahneman and Angus Deaton. Their 2010 study sent shockwaves through the financial world. They found that emotional well-being, the frequency, and intensity of experiences of joy, fascination, anxiety, sadness, anger, and affection, rises with income, but only up to an annual salary of about $75,000. Beyond that, additional income buys life satisfaction, but not happiness.

This finding leads us to an intriguing concept: the hedonic treadmill. Imagine running on a treadmill , no matter how fast you go, you stay in the same place. Similarly, as people accumulate more wealth, they adapt to their new circumstances. The initial thrill of a pay raise or a luxury purchase quickly fades, leaving them yearning for the next bump in status or income.

But the evidence doesn't stop there. Let's jet across the Pacific to Japan, where a fascinating economic phenomenon unfolded. Between 1958 and 1987, Japan experienced a fivefold increase in real income. Yet, over this same period, the country saw no significant increase in reported life satisfaction. This paradox, known as the Easterlin Paradox, has been observed in numerous countries, further challenging the money-happiness equation.

Transitioning from macro to micro, let's consider the lottery, the ultimate financial windfall. Surely, lottery winners must be the happiest people on Earth, right? Not so fast. A famous study by Brickman, Coates, and Janoff-Bulman found that while lottery winners experienced initial euphoria, they quickly returned to their baseline levels of happiness. In some cases, they even reported lower life satisfaction due to decreased enjoyment of ordinary pleasures.

On the flip side, research has shown that experiences, rather than material possessions, tend to make people happier. A study by Thomas Gilovich and Amit Kumar found that experiential purchases, like concerts, travel, or learning a new skill, provide more lasting happiness than material goods. This suggests that how we spend our money may be more important than how much we have.

Moreover, the pursuit of wealth often comes at a cost. A survey by the American Psychological Association found that money is a significant source of stress for 72% of Americans. High-income individuals regularly report higher levels of stress and less time for personal relationships and leisure activities, crucial components of happiness.

So, what can we learn from all this evidence? The relationship between money and happiness is far more complex than a simple equation. While financial security is important, blindly chasing wealth may lead us down a path of diminishing returns.
To help you apply these insights to your own life, try this reflective exercise:

1. List your top five sources of happiness from the past month.
2. For each item, note whether it was related to a material purchase or an experience.
3. Estimate the cost of each item or experience.
4. Reflect on the relationship between the cost and the happiness derived. Are your most expensive items always your happiest?

This exercise can help you become more conscious of what truly brings you joy, potentially reshaping how you allocate your resources in the future.

As we move forward, we'll explore more nuanced ways of thinking about money and its role in our lives. Remember, questioning the money-happiness equation isn't about rejecting financial success. Rather, it's about understanding its limitations and finding a more balanced approach to well-being.

Chapter 2: The Wealth Psychology Minefields

Picture a glittering Las Vegas casino floor. Amidst the cacophony of slot machines and cheering gamblers, a well-dressed man places an audacious bet. His eyes gleam with anticipation, heart racing as the roulette wheel spins. This scene, rife with risk and potential reward, mirrors the psychological landscape we navigate when dealing with wealth.

Welcome to the treacherous terrain of wealth psychology, where hidden pitfalls and cognitive booby traps lurk beneath the surface of our financial decisions. Here, we'll don our psychological miner's helmets and venture into the dark recesses of the human mind, illuminating the subtle yet powerful forces that shape our relationship with money.

In this chapter, we'll uncover the behavioral money traps that ensnare even the savviest investors. From the siren song of sunk costs to the dizzying allure of get-rich-quick schemes, we'll explore how our brains often betray us when it comes to financial decision-making. You'll discover why that "can't-miss" investment opportunity might be more mirage than oasis, and how our emotions can lead us astray in the high-stakes world of personal finance.

But our expedition doesn't stop there. We'll also delve into the fascinating paradox of pursuit: how the very act of chasing wealth can sometimes push happiness further from our grasp. It's a psychological tightrope walk, where the promise of future contentment frequently overshadows present joy.

As we navigate these minefields, you'll gain insight into your own financial behaviors and biases. You might find yourself nodding in recognition as we dissect common money mistakes, or raising an eyebrow at the surprising ways wealth can warp our perceptions and priorities.

By the end of this chapter, you'll be equipped with a mental map of the wealth psychology landscape. You'll understand the cognitive tripwires that can derail your financial well-being, and have strategies to sidestep these hazards. Most importantly, you'll gain a deeper appreciation for the complex interplay between money, mind, and happiness.

So, tighten your bootlaces and brace yourself for an eye-opening journey through the minefields of wealth psychology. It's time to defuse some financial fallacies and clear a path towards a healthier, more balanced relationship with money.

2.1: Behavioral Money Traps

Meet Sarah, a savvy marketing executive who prides herself on her financial acumen. Yet, last month, she found herself pouring another $1,000 into a failing investment, unable to let go. Sarah had fallen into one of the most common behavioral money traps: the sunk cost fallacy. Her story serves as a perfect entry point into our exploration of the psychological pitfalls that often ensnare us in our financial decisions.

Behavioral money traps are cognitive biases that lead us to make irrational financial choices. These mental quirks, hardwired into our brains through evolution, once helped our ancestors survive in a world of scarcity. Today, however, they frequently misfire in our complex financial landscape.

Let's start with the sunk cost fallacy that snared Sarah. This trap occurs when we continue a behavior or endeavor due to previously invested resources, even when it's no longer rational to do so. It's why we finish a movie we're not enjoying or, more damaging, hold onto a plummeting stock hoping it will rebound.

Moving from sunk costs, we encounter another treacherous terrain: loss aversion. Studies show that the pain of losing is psychologically about twice as powerful as the pleasure of gaining. This asymmetry leads to overly conservative investment strategies or, paradoxically, risky behaviors to recoup losses. Think of the gambler who doubles down after a string of losses, desperately trying to break even.

But the rabbit hole of behavioral traps goes deeper. Consider the anchoring bias, where we rely too heavily on the first piece of information encountered when making decisions. In financial contexts, this could mean fixating on a stock's past high price or being swayed by the first house price we see in a new neighborhood.

Transitioning to another cognitive quirk, we find the overconfidence bias. This is the tendency to overestimate our own abilities, including our financial acumen. It's what leads amateur investors to believe they can consistently beat the market or entrepreneurs to overlook critical flaws in their business plans.

Closely related is the illusion of control, where we overestimate our ability to control events. In finance, this might manifest as thinking we can time the market or predict economic trends with certainty.

Let's not forget the recency bias, our tendency to place too much importance on recent events and ignore historical patterns. This can lead to chasing the latest hot stock or panic-selling during market downturns, ignoring the long-term perspective.

Lastly, we have the herd mentality, our inclination to follow the crowd. In the financial world, this can result in bubbles and crashes as investors pile into or flee from assets en masse, often against their better judgment.

Understanding these traps is crucial, but how do we avoid them? Here are some strategies:

1. Awareness is the first step. Recognizing these biases in action can help us pause and reconsider our decisions.

2. Seek diverse perspectives. Consulting with others can help counteract our individual biases.

3. Use data and analysis. Hard numbers can provide a reality check against our emotional impulses.
4. Implement cooling-off periods. Delay major financial decisions to allow emotions to settle.

5. Develop and stick to a long-term financial plan. This can help resist short-term temptations and biases.

To help internalize these concepts, try this exercise:

1. Reflect on a recent financial decision you regret.
2. Identify which behavioral trap(s) might have influenced your choice.
3. Write down how you could have approached the situation differently, armed with this new knowledge.
4. Create a personal checklist of questions to ask yourself before making future financial decisions, designed to counteract these biases.

By acknowledging and actively working to counteract these behavioral money traps, we can make more rational, beneficial financial decisions. Remember, even the most financially savvy among us are susceptible to these psychological quirks. The key is to remain vigilant, self-aware, and committed to continuous learning and improvement in our financial lives.

2.2: The Pursuit That Appends Happiness

Meet Tom, a 35-year-old software engineer who's been chasing the next big promotion for years. He's certain that once he reaches the coveted senior management position, he'll finally be content. Yet, with each step up the corporate ladder, Tom finds his happiness always seems to be just out of reach. Tom's story illustrates a common psychological phenomenon: the hedonic treadmill.

The hedonic treadmill, or hedonic adaptation, refers to the human tendency to swiftly return to a baseline level of happiness, even after experiencing significant positive or negative life events. This concept is key to understanding why the pursuit of wealth frequently falls short of providing the enduring happiness that many anticipate.

Let's break this down further. When we acquire something new—be it a raise, a new car, or a bigger house—we experience a temporary boost in happiness. However, we quickly adapt to our new circumstances, and our happiness levels return to their baseline. It's as if we're running on a treadmill; no matter how fast we run, we stay in the same place happiness-wise.

This phenomenon isn't limited to material acquisitions. Even major life achievements, like landing that dream job or reaching a significant financial milestone, are subject to hedonic adaptation. The initial euphoria fades, and we find ourselves seeking the next big thing to make us happy.

Consider the case of lottery winners. A famous study by Brickman, Coates, and Janoff-Bulman found that while lottery winners experienced initial elation, they quickly returned to their baseline levels of happiness. In some cases, they even reported lower life satisfaction due to decreased enjoyment of ordinary pleasures.

Transitioning from individual experiences to broader societal trends, we see this pattern replicated on a larger scale. Despite significant increases in average income and standard of living over the past several decades in many countries, overall happiness levels have remained relatively stable. This phenomenon, known as the Easterlin Paradox, further underscores the complex relationship between wealth and happiness.

So, why does this happen? One explanation lies in the concept of relative wealth. As our wealth increases, so do our expectations and desires. We compare ourselves to a new peer group, and suddenly, what we have doesn't seem as satisfying. This constant upward comparison can lead to a never-ending cycle of pursuit without lasting satisfaction.

Moreover, the pursuit of wealth often comes at a cost. Many high-earners report higher levels of stress, less time for personal relationships, and reduced leisure time - all crucial components of happiness. The irony is that in chasing the means to happiness (money), we frequently sacrifice the very things that truly make us happy.

This isn't to say that money is irrelevant to happiness. Financial security certainly contributes to well-being by alleviating stress and providing opportunities. However, beyond a certain point - what researchers call the "satiation point" - additional income has diminishing returns on happiness.

How, then, can we break free from this cycle? Here are some strategies:

1. Practice gratitude: Regularly acknowledging what you already have can counteract the tendency to always want more.

2. Focus on experiences rather than possessions: Research shows that experiential purchases tend to provide more lasting happiness than material ones.

3. Invest in relationships: Strong social connections are consistently linked to higher levels of happiness.

4. Find purpose beyond wealth: Engage in activities that provide meaning and fulfillment, regardless of their financial reward.

5. Set intrinsic goals: Aim for personal growth, strong relationships, and community contribution rather than extrinsic goals like wealth and status.

To help internalize these concepts, try this exercise:

1. List five things you believe would make you happier if you had more money.
2. For each item, ask yourself: Is it the item itself that would bring happiness, or what it represents?
3. Brainstorm alternative ways to achieve the underlying desire without spending money.
4. Commit to trying one of these alternatives in the next week.

By understanding the hedonic treadmill and actively working to counteract its effects, we can cultivate a more sustainable and genuine sense of happiness. Remember, true contentment often lies not in the endless pursuit of more, but in learning to appreciate and make the most of what we already have.

Chapter 3: When Money Changes People

Picture a modest lottery ticket, clutched in trembling hands. The numbers align, and suddenly, an ordinary life is catapulted into extraordinary wealth. It's a dream shared by millions, but what happens when that dream becomes reality? How does a sudden influx of money reshape not just bank accounts, but the very essence of who we are?

In this chapter, we embark on a fascinating journey into the transformative power of wealth. We'll peel back the layers of human psychology to reveal how financial windfalls can alter personalities, relationships, and fundamental values. From rags-to-riches stories that inspire to cautionary tales of fortunes squandered, we'll explore the myriad ways money molds the human experience.

Our exploration begins with the immediate effects of newfound wealth. We'll delve into the euphoria of financial freedom and the unexpected anxieties that often accompany it. How does instant affluence impact decision-making, risk tolerance, and self-perception? These questions set the stage for our deeper dive into long-term changes.

As we progress, we'll examine how wealth can reshape social dynamics. Friends become potential moochers, family relationships strain under new expectations, and the world seems to view the newly rich through a different lens. We'll uncover the isolation that can paradoxically accompany financial success and the challenges of maintaining authentic connections in a money-centric world.

But our investigation doesn't stop at personal relationships. We'll also scrutinize how wealth influences broader societal interactions. Does money truly corrupt, or does it simply amplify existing traits? We'll look at studies on empathy, generosity, and ethical decision-making among the affluent, challenging common assumptions and uncovering surprising truths.

Throughout this chapter, we'll weave together scientific research, real-life anecdotes, and expert insights to paint a comprehensive picture of wealth's transformative effects. You'll gain a nuanced understanding of how money changes people, for better and for worse.

By the end of this exploration, you'll be equipped with valuable insights into the psychological impact of wealth. Whether you're dreaming of striking it rich or simply seeking to understand the wealthy world around you, this chapter offers a roadmap to navigating the complex terrain where money and human nature intersect.

So, prepare yourself for an enlightening journey ahead. It's time to unravel the mysteries of how cold, hard cash can reshape the warm, complex landscape of human behavior.

3.1: Affluence's Identity Impacts

Meet Mark, a 32-year-old teacher who recently inherited a substantial sum from a distant relative. Overnight, his net worth skyrocketed from modest to millions. At first, Mark felt elated, but soon he found himself grappling with an unexpected question: "Who am I now?" "Mark's story provides an ideal starting point for our exploration of the profound effects sudden wealth can have on one's sense of identity."

The influence of affluence on identity is a complex interplay of psychological, social, and economic factors. To understand this phenomenon, let's break it down into key components:

1. Self-Perception Shift:
When individuals experience a significant increase in wealth, their self-image often undergoes a dramatic transformation. Mark, for

instance, always saw himself as a hardworking, middle-class professional. Now, he struggles to reconcile his new financial status with his long-held self-perception. This internal conflict can lead to what psychologists call "sudden wealth syndrome," characterized by feelings of guilt, anxiety, and isolation.

2. Social Identity Recalibration:
Wealth doesn't just change how we see ourselves; it alters how others perceive us too. Mark noticed that his colleagues and friends started treating him differently once news of his inheritance spread. Some became overly deferential, while others grew distant. This shift in social dynamics can force newly wealthy individuals to reevaluate their place in their social circles and even in society at large.

3. Value System Challenge:
Money has the power to test our core values. Mark, who always prided himself on his frugality and simplicity, now faces the temptation of luxury and excess. This internal tug-of-war between old values and new possibilities is a common struggle for those experiencing sudden wealth.

4. Purpose and Meaning Redefinition:
With financial security comes the freedom to pursue new goals. However, this freedom can also lead to a crisis of purpose. Mark, no longer bound by financial necessity to his teaching job, questions whether he should continue in his profession or explore other avenues. This search for new meaning is a crucial aspect of the identity shift that accompanies sudden wealth.

5. Relationship Dynamics Alteration:
Wealth can act as a magnifying glass on relationships, amplifying both positive and negative aspects. Mark finds some friendships strengthening as he's able to be more generous, while others strain

under the weight of changed circumstances and expectations. Family relationships, too, can undergo significant changes, with money often bringing latent tensions to the surface.

6. Impostor Syndrome:
Many newly wealthy individuals, like Mark, experience a form of impostor syndrome. They may feel undeserving of their wealth or worry that others will see them as frauds. This psychological phenomenon can significantly impact self-esteem and decision-making.

Transitioning from these impacts, it's crucial to understand that navigating this identity shift is a process, not an event. It requires conscious effort and, frequently, professional guidance. Financial advisors and therapists specializing in sudden wealth syndrome can provide invaluable support during this transition.

To help readers apply these concepts to their own lives, consider the following exercise:

1. Reflect on your current identity: List five key aspects of how you see yourself.
2. Imagine a significant increase in wealth: How might each of these aspects change?
3. Identify potential challenges: What conflicts might arise between your current and potential future self?
4. Plan for continuity: List three core values or aspects of your identity you'd want to maintain regardless of wealth.
5. Envision positive change: How could you use newfound resources to enhance your identity in meaningful ways?

By engaging in this reflective exercise, you can prepare yourself mentally for potential wealth increases, ensuring that your core identity remains stable amidst financial changes.

To wrap up, while sudden wealth can indeed reshape our identities, it doesn't have to redefine us entirely. By staying grounded in our core values, maintaining meaningful relationships, and seeking purpose beyond material gain, we can navigate the choppy waters of affluence's identity impacts. The key lies in viewing wealth as a tool for enhancing our authentic selves, rather than a force that fundamentally alters who we are.

3.2: Relationship Hazards of Riches

Let's meet Emma, a successful entrepreneur who recently sold her tech startup for millions. While she expected her newfound wealth to enhance her life, she's now grappling with unexpected challenges in her relationships. Emma's story serves as a compelling introduction to the complex ways in which wealth can affect our connections with others.

Wealth, while often viewed as a solution to many problems, can introduce a unique set of challenges to relationships. These challenges can be grouped into several key categories:

1. Trust Issues:
One of the most immediate impacts of wealth on relationships is the introduction of doubt. Emma found herself questioning the motives of new acquaintances and even long-time friends. Are they interested in her as a person, or her bank account? This constant scrutiny can lead to paranoia and isolation, making it difficult to form genuine connections.

2. Power Dynamics Shift:
In existing relationships, a sudden influx of wealth can upset the balance of power. Emma noticed that her opinions suddenly carried more weight in her friend group, even on topics where she wasn't an

expert. This shift can lead to resentment from others and discomfort for the wealthy individual.

3. Expectations and Obligations:

With great wealth comes great expectation, often from family and friends. Emma found herself inundated with requests for financial assistance, investment in business ideas, and expensive gifts. These expectations can strain relationships and create a sense of obligation that wasn't present before.

4. Lifestyle Incompatibility:

As Emma's lifestyle changed to accommodate her new financial status, she found herself drifting apart from old friends. Differences in spending habits, leisure activities, and even conversation topics created a widening gap. This incompatibility can lead to the loss of long-standing relationships.

5. Envy and Resentment:

Even the most well-intentioned friends and family members may struggle with feelings of envy. Emma noticed subtle changes in some relationships, backhanded compliments, passive-aggressive remarks about her spending, or a general coolness. These negative emotions can poison previously positive relationships.

6. Difficulty in Forming New, Authentic Relationships:

For the newly wealthy, forming new relationships can be challenging. Emma struggled to discern whether new acquaintances were interested in her or her wealth. This uncertainty can lead to a reluctance to open up and create deep connections.

Transitioning from these challenges, it's important to note that while wealth can complicate relationships, it doesn't inevitably destroy them. With awareness and effort, it's possible to maintain healthy connections and form new, genuine bonds.

Here are some strategies to navigate these relationship hazards:

1. Maintain Transparency: Open communication about your financial situation and boundaries can prevent misunderstandings and unrealistic expectations.

2. Stay Grounded: Remember your values and the relationships that mattered to you before wealth. Aim to uphold authenticity in your interactions.

3. Set Clear Boundaries: Establish limits on financial assistance and be consistent in applying them across relationships.

4. Seek Like-Minded Individuals: Connect with others who share your values, regardless of their financial status.

5. Practice Empathy: Try to understand the perspective of friends and family who may be struggling financially.

6. Consider Philanthropy: Engaging in charitable activities can provide a sense of purpose and connect you with others who share your values.

To help readers apply these concepts, consider the following exercise:

1. Relationship Inventory: List your key relationships and how wealth has affected each one.
2. Boundary Setting: Write down specific financial boundaries you want to establish in your relationships.
3. Value Alignment: Identify three core values you want to maintain in your relationships, regardless of wealth.
4. Communication Plan: Draft a script for discussing your financial situation and boundaries with a close friend or family member.

5. Authentic Connection: Plan an activity with a friend that doesn't involve spending money.

By engaging in this reflective exercise, you can proactively address potential relationship challenges that come with wealth.

To sum up, while wealth can indeed introduce hazards to relationships, it also provides opportunities for growth and deeper connections. By staying true to your values, communicating openly, and setting clear boundaries, you can navigate these choppy waters and maintain meaningful relationships. Remember, true wealth lies not just in your bank account, but in the quality of your connections with others.

Chapter 4: Cultural Perspectives on Money and Happiness

Money speaks, but its accent varies across the globe. From the bustling markets of Marrakech to the gleaming skyscrapers of Tokyo, the relationship between wealth and well-being takes on unique hues, shaped by centuries of tradition, philosophy, and social norms. In this chapter, we embark on a worldwide journey to explore how different cultures view the intricate dance between financial success and personal fulfillment.

Our exploration begins with a fundamental question: Is the pursuit of happiness through monetary gain a universal human trait, or a product of specific cultural conditioning? To answer this, we'll delve into the rich tapestry of global perspectives, examining how various societies define wealth, success, and contentment.

We'll start by contrasting Eastern and Western philosophies on money and happiness. While many Western cultures often equate financial success with personal achievement, Eastern traditions frequently emphasize spiritual wealth and inner peace over material accumulation. This dichotomy sets the stage for our deeper investigation into cultural nuances.

Our journey will then take us through diverse cultural landscapes, each offering unique insights:

1. We'll explore the Scandinavian concept of "lagom" - the art of balanced living - and how it shapes attitudes towards wealth and contentment.

2. We'll examine the African philosophy of "ubuntu," which prioritizes community well-being over individual wealth, and its impact on personal happiness.

3. We'll investigate the Japanese principle of "ikigai," which seeks to find purpose at the intersection of passion, profession, vocation, and mission.

4. We'll look at how the American Dream has evolved and its influence on global perceptions of money and success.

As we traverse these cultural perspectives, we'll uncover surprising similarities and stark differences in how societies around the world perceive the relationship between money and happiness. We'll challenge our own preconceptions and gain a more nuanced understanding of this universal yet deeply personal topic.

By the end of this chapter, you'll have a panoramic view of how culture shapes our understanding of wealth and well-being. This knowledge will not only broaden your perspective but also provide valuable insights into navigating our increasingly interconnected global economy.

So, fasten your seatbelts and prepare for a thought-provoking journey around the world. It's time to discover how different cultures answer the age-old question: Can money buy happiness?

4.1: Eastern vs. Western Views on Wealth and Contentment

Meet Aiko and Sarah, two successful professionals in their mid-thirties. Aiko, raised in Japan, and Sarah, from the United States, both work for multinational corporations. Despite their similar career paths, their perspectives on wealth and happiness couldn't be more different. Their contrasting views serve as a perfect starting point to explore the divergent Eastern and Western approaches to money and contentment.

Western Perspective:
In many Western cultures, particularly in the United States, wealth is often equated with success and happiness. This view is deeply rooted in

the concept of individualism and the "American Dream." Sarah, our American example, sees her rising income as a direct measure of her personal achievement. She believes that with more money, she can buy experiences and possessions that will make her happier.

Key aspects of the Western view include:

1. Material Success: There's a strong emphasis on accumulating wealth and material possessions.
2. Individual Achievement: Personal success is highly valued and often measured in financial terms.
3. Conspicuous Consumption: Displaying wealth through purchases is seen as a sign of success.
4. Future-Oriented: There's a focus on working hard now for future rewards.

Eastern Perspective:

In contrast, many Eastern cultures, influenced by philosophies like Buddhism, Taoism, and Confucianism, frequently view wealth and happiness through a different lens. Aiko, our Japanese professional, while appreciating financial stability, doesn't see it as the primary source of contentment. She places more value on harmony, balance, and spiritual well-being.

Key aspects of the Eastern view include:

1. Spiritual Wealth: Inner peace and spiritual growth are often prioritized over material wealth.
2. Collective Well-being: The focus is more on community harmony than individual success.
3. Moderation: There's an emphasis on finding balance rather than excess.

4. Present-Oriented: Living at the moment is regularly valued over future gains.

To illustrate these differences, let's look at how Aiko and Sarah approach a pay raise:

Sarah sees her raise as a validation of her hard work and immediately plans how to upgrade her lifestyle. She considers buying a bigger house or a luxury car, seeing these as rewards for her success and potential sources of happiness.

Aiko, while appreciating the raise, doesn't view it as a reason to change her lifestyle dramatically. Instead, she might use some of the extra money for a family vacation, save more for the future, or donate to her community. Her focus remains on maintaining balance in her life.

It's important to note that these are generalizations, and individual views within each culture can vary widely. Moreover, with globalization, these perspectives are increasingly blending and evolving.

The impact of these cultural views on personal happiness and societal well-being is significant:

1. Work-Life Balance: Western cultures often struggle with work-life balance, while many Eastern cultures prioritize it.
2. Stress Levels: The constant pursuit of more in Western cultures can lead to higher stress levels.
3. Community Bonds: Eastern cultures' focus on collective well-being regularly results in stronger community ties.
4. Innovation and Growth: The Western emphasis on individual achievement can drive innovation and economic growth.

Transitioning from these observations, it's crucial to understand that neither view is inherently superior. Both have their strengths and weaknesses. The key is to find a personal balance that aligns with your values and leads to genuine contentment.

To help readers apply these concepts to their own lives, consider the following exercise:

1. Values Assessment: List your top five values. Are they more aligned with Eastern or Western perspectives?
2. Contentment Reflection: Recall three moments when you felt truly content. Were they related to material wealth or other factors?
3. Cultural Influence: Identify three ways your culture influences your view of money and happiness.
4. Balance Plan: Create a plan to incorporate one aspect from the opposing cultural view into your life.
5. Gratitude Practice: Start a daily gratitude journal, focusing on non-material sources of happiness.

By engaging in this reflective exercise, you can gain insights into your own cultural biases and potentially broaden your perspective on wealth and contentment.

To wrap up, understanding these diverse cultural views on wealth and happiness can enrich our own approach to life. By cherry-picking the most beneficial aspects from both Eastern and Western philosophies, we can craft a more balanced, fulfilling relationship with money and happiness. Remember, true wealth isn't just about the numbers in your bank account, but about creating a life rich in meaning, relationships, and personal growth.

4.2: Case Study: Bhutan's Gross National Happiness vs. GDP

In the heart of the Himalayas lies a small kingdom that has captured the world's attention not for its economic might, but for its unique approach to measuring national progress. Bhutan, with its population of just over

750,000, has pioneered the concept of Gross National Happiness (GNH) as an alternative to the widely used Gross Domestic Product (GDP). This case study explores how Bhutan's innovative approach challenges conventional notions of national success and offers insights into the relationship between wealth and well-being.

Let's start with Dorji, a 45-year-old farmer from central Bhutan. Unlike his counterparts in many developing nations, Dorji doesn't measure his success solely by his income. Instead, he considers factors like his community relationships, the health of his environment, and his spiritual well-being. This holistic view of personal success mirrors Bhutan's national approach to progress.

Bhutan's GNH concept was introduced in 1972 by the fourth King of Bhutan, Jigme Singye Wangchuck. It was a bold declaration that the happiness and well-being of the people should take precedence over material growth. This philosophy has since guided Bhutan's development policies and has been formalized into a comprehensive index.

The GNH Index comprises nine domains:

1. Psychological well-being
2. Health
3. Education
4. Time use
5. Cultural diversity and resilience
6. Good governance
7. Community vitality
8. Ecological diversity and resilience
9. Living standards

Each domain is given equal weight, reflecting the belief that all aspects are crucial for overall happiness and well-being. This multidimensional approach stands in stark contrast to GDP, which focuses solely on economic output.

To understand the practical implications of this approach, let's compare two scenarios:

Scenario 1: A new factory is proposed in Dorji's village. It would significantly increase the local GDP but would also pollute the nearby river and disrupt traditional community gatherings.

Scenario 2: A community center is built, slightly increasing GDP through construction costs. It provides a space for cultural events, education programs, and community meetings.

In a purely GDP-focused system, Scenario 1 might be favored for its economic impact. However, under the GNH framework, Scenario 2 would likely be preferred as it positively impacts multiple domains of happiness without compromising others.

This approach has led to some remarkable outcomes for Bhutan:

1. Environmental Protection: Bhutan is the world's only carbon-negative country, with over 70% of its land under forest cover.
2. Cultural Preservation: Traditional arts, crafts, and customs are actively promoted and preserved.
3. Universal Healthcare: Bhutan provides free healthcare to all its citizens.
4. Education: The country has achieved near-universal primary education.

However, the GNH approach is not without challenges:

1. Economic Growth: Bhutan's GDP growth has been slower compared to some of its neighbors.

2. Measurement Complexity: Quantifying happiness and well-being is inherently more complex than measuring economic output.

3. Global Integration: Balancing traditional values with the pressures of globalization remains an ongoing challenge.

Despite these challenges, Bhutan's approach has sparked global interest. Countries like New Zealand, Scotland, and the United Arab Emirates have begun incorporating well-being measures into their national policies, inspired in part by Bhutan's example.

Transitioning from Bhutan's national policy to personal application, we can draw valuable lessons from the GNH approach. It encourages us to view success and progress through a more holistic lens, considering not just financial gains but also personal well-being, community relationships, and environmental sustainability.

To help readers apply these concepts to their own lives, consider the following exercise:

1. Personal GNH Index: Create your own happiness index by listing 5-7 domains that contribute to your overall well-being (e.g., health, relationships, personal growth, financial security, etc.).

2. Domain Assessment: Rate your current satisfaction in each domain on a scale of 1-10.

3. Holistic Goal Setting: Set one goal for each domain that would improve your overall well-being, not just your financial situation.

4. Balance Check: Before making a major decision, consider how it would impact each of your personal GNH domains, not just your finances.

5. Community Contribution: Identify one way you can contribute to your community's well-being this week.

By engaging in this reflective exercise, you can start to cultivate a more balanced approach to personal success and happiness, inspired by Bhutan's national philosophy.

To sum up, Bhutan's Gross National Happiness index offers a compelling alternative to GDP-centric measures of progress. While it may not be a perfect system, it challenges us to reconsider what truly constitutes success and well-being, both on a national and personal level. As we navigate an increasingly complex world, Bhutan's example reminds us that true wealth encompasses far more than just monetary value.

4.3: How Religious and Philosophical Traditions Shape Money Attitudes

Money, often considered a universal language, is spoken with different dialects across the world's religions and philosophies. These belief systems profoundly influence how individuals and societies view wealth, shaping attitudes towards earning, spending, saving, and sharing money. Let's explore how major religious and philosophical traditions mold our relationship with finance.

To illustrate this, we'll follow the stories of four individuals from different backgrounds:

1. Sarah - a Protestant Christian from the United States
2. Rahul - a Hindu from India
3. Aisha - a Muslim from Indonesia
4. Mei - a Buddhist from China

Christianity:

Sarah's Protestant upbringing emphasizes the concept of stewardship. She believes that wealth is a gift from God, to be used responsibly and shared with others. The Protestant work ethic, which links hard work with moral virtue, influences her approach to earning money.

Key Christian money attitudes:
- Work is a calling and should be pursued diligently
- Tithing (giving a portion of income to the church) is important
- Wealth should be used to help others
- Excessive materialism is discouraged

Hinduism:

Rahul's Hindu background introduces him to the concept of 'artha' (material wealth) as one of life's legitimate goals, balanced with spiritual pursuits. He views wealth as part of the natural order but believes it should be acquired ethically.

Key Hindu money attitudes:
- Wealth is one of life's goals, but not the ultimate one
- Money should be earned through ethical practices.
- Charity (dana) is an important spiritual practice
- Detachment from material possessions is valued

Islam:

Aisha's Islamic faith provides clear guidelines on financial matters. She avoids interest-based transactions and believes in the importance of 'zakat' (obligatory charity).

Key Islamic money attitudes:
- Interest (riba) is prohibited
- Wealth should be gained through halal (permissible) means
- Zakat is a religious duty
- Moderation in spending is encouraged

Buddhism:

Mei's Buddhist beliefs emphasize detachment from material possessions. She sees the pursuit of wealth as a potential source of suffering if not approached with the right mindset.

Key Buddhist money attitudes:
- Attachment to wealth can lead to suffering
- Generosity is a key virtue
- Mindful consumption is encouraged
- The middle way between asceticism and indulgence is ideal

These religious perspectives intertwine with philosophical traditions to further shape money attitudes:

Confucianism, prevalent in East Asian cultures, emphasizes social harmony and filial piety. This translates to financial practices like saving for the future and supporting family members.

Western philosophy, influenced by thinkers like Adam Smith, often emphasizes individual rights and free-market principles, shaping capitalist attitudes towards money.

The interplay between these religious and philosophical traditions creates a complex tapestry of money attitudes worldwide. For instance, Sarah's Protestant work ethic might align with capitalist principles, while Mei's Buddhist detachment could conflict with consumerist trends.

As our world becomes increasingly interconnected, these diverse perspectives often clash and blend. Consider a multinational company operating in various countries: it must navigate these different money attitudes to effectively manage its global workforce and customer base.

Understanding these varied perspectives can help us in several ways:

1. Personal Finance: Recognizing the roots of our money attitudes can help us make more conscious financial decisions.
2. Business: Companies can tailor their products and marketing strategies to align with local money attitudes.
3. Policy Making: Governments can create more effective economic policies by considering cultural attitudes towards money.
4. Global Understanding: Appreciating diverse views on wealth can foster better international relations and cooperation.

To help apply these concepts to your own life, consider the following exercises:

1. Money Attitude Reflection: Write down five of your core beliefs about money. Try to trace the origins of these beliefs - are they influenced by your religious or philosophical background?

2. Cultural Comparison: Research money attitudes in a culture different from your own. Identify three practices or beliefs that differ from yours.

3. Value Alignment: List your top five values. How do your current financial habits align with these values? Identify areas where you could bring your money practices more in line with your core beliefs.

4. Mindful Spending Challenge: For one week, before each purchase, pause and reflect on whether it aligns with your personal values and beliefs about money.

5. Generosity Practice: Choose a cause that aligns with your beliefs and set aside a portion of your income for charitable giving.

By engaging in these exercises, you can gain a deeper understanding of your own money attitudes and how they've been shaped by religious and philosophical traditions.

To wrap up, our attitudes towards money are deeply ingrained, often stemming from long-standing religious and philosophical traditions. By understanding these influences, we can make more conscious financial decisions that align with our values and beliefs. Moreover, appreciating the diversity of money attitudes globally can foster greater empathy and effectiveness in our increasingly interconnected world. Remember, there's no universally "right" way to view money, the key is to find an approach that balances financial health with your personal beliefs and values.

4.4: The Impact of Collectivist vs. Individualist Societies on Wealth Perception

The way societies view wealth is deeply influenced by their cultural orientation towards collectivism or individualism. These contrasting perspectives shape not only how people perceive and pursue wealth, but also how they define success and happiness. Let's explore this fascinating divide through the lens of two fictional characters: Emma from the United States (an individualist society) and Hiroshi from Japan (a collectivist society).

Individualist Societies:

In individualist cultures like the United States, the United Kingdom, and Australia, personal achievement and self-reliance are highly valued. Emma, our American example, views wealth primarily as a personal accomplishment and a means to express her individuality.

Key characteristics of wealth perception in individualist societies:

1. **Personal Success:** Wealth is often seen as a direct reflection of one's abilities and efforts.
2. **Financial Independence:** There's a strong emphasis on being self-sufficient and not relying on others.

3. Conspicuous Consumption: Displaying wealth through purchases is more socially acceptable and even encouraged.
4. Risk-Taking: There's generally more acceptance of entrepreneurial risk in pursuit of personal wealth.

For Emma, starting her own business is not just about making money; it's a way to prove herself and achieve personal freedom. She's comfortable taking risks and doesn't shy away from showcasing her success through her lifestyle choices.

Collectivist Societies:

In contrast, collectivist cultures like those found in many Asian, African, and Latin American countries prioritize group harmony and interdependence. Hiroshi, our Japanese example, sees wealth more in terms of its benefits to his family and community.

Key characteristics of wealth perception in collectivist societies:

1. Family and Community Focus: Wealth is often viewed in terms of how it can benefit the extended family or community.
2. Social Harmony: There's a stronger emphasis on avoiding social disparity and maintaining group cohesion.
3. Modest Display: Overt displays of wealth may be seen as inappropriate or boastful.
4. Long-term Orientation: There's frequently a greater focus on long-term financial stability over short-term gains.

Hiroshi, despite being successful in his career, is more likely to live modestly and prioritize saving for his children's education or his parents' retirement over luxury purchases for himself.

The impact of these cultural differences on wealth perception is profound and far-reaching:

1. Career Choices: In individualist societies, career choices might be based more on personal passion and potential earnings. In collectivist societies, consideration of family expectations and community needs often play a larger role.

2. Spending Habits: Individualist cultures might see more spending on personal luxuries, while collectivist cultures might prioritize spending on family events or community contributions.

3. Entrepreneurship: Individualist societies often have higher rates of entrepreneurship, as striking out on one's own is more culturally encouraged.

4. Wealth Distribution: Collectivist societies might have more informal wealth distribution within extended families, while individualist societies might rely more on formal charitable giving.

5. Retirement Planning: In collectivist societies, there might be a greater expectation of family support in old age, while individualist societies emphasize personal retirement savings.

These differences can lead to misunderstandings in our globalized world. For instance, a Western company might struggle to motivate employees in a collectivist culture with individual performance bonuses, as these might disrupt group harmony. Conversely, a collectivist approach to decision-making might frustrate workers from individualist cultures who value personal autonomy.

However, it's important to note that these are general tendencies, and individual variations exist within each culture. Moreover, as the world becomes more interconnected, many societies are adopting a blend of individualist and collectivist values.

Understanding these cultural differences can be invaluable in various contexts:

1. International Business: Companies can tailor their management styles and product offerings to align with local cultural values.
2. Personal Finance: Individuals can better understand their own financial behaviors and biases.
3. Policy Making: Governments can create more effective economic policies by considering cultural attitudes towards wealth.
4. Cross-Cultural Relationships: Understanding these differences can help in navigating personal and professional relationships across cultures.

To help apply these concepts to your own life, consider the following exercises:

1. Cultural Self-Assessment: Reflect on your own culture's tendencies. List five ways your society's individualist or collectivist orientation has influenced your view of wealth.

2. Value Prioritization: Rank the following values from most to least important to you: personal achievement, family obligation, community contribution, individual expression, social harmony. How does this ranking align with individualist or collectivist perspectives?

3. Decision-Making Exercise: Think of a major financial decision you need to make. List the factors you're considering. How many of these factors are focused on personal benefit versus family or community benefit?

4. Cross-Cultural Perspective Taking: Choose a financial behavior that differs between individualist and collectivist cultures (e.g., displaying wealth, supporting extended family). Try to articulate the perspective of someone from the opposite cultural orientation.

5. Blended Approach Brainstorm: Identify one individualist and one collectivist approach to wealth that resonate with you. How could you incorporate both into your financial life?

By engaging with these exercises, you can gain deeper insights into how cultural orientations shape wealth perceptions and potentially broaden your own financial perspective.

To sum up, the divide between collectivist and individualist societies significantly impacts how wealth is perceived, pursued, and utilized. By understanding these cultural differences, we can navigate our global economy more effectively, make more informed financial decisions, and perhaps even strike a balance between personal aspirations and community well-being. Remember, there's no universally "correct" way to view wealth - the key is to understand diverse perspectives and find an approach that aligns with both your personal values and the realities of your cultural context.

Chapter 5: Economic Factors and the Happiness Equation

Money can't buy happiness, or can it? This age-old adage has been debated, dissected, and deliberated upon for generations. As we dive into Chapter 5, we're about to unravel the complex tapestry that interweaves economic factors with our sense of well-being. Buckle up, because we're embarking on a journey that will challenge your preconceptions and shed light on the elusive happiness equation.

Picture this: two individuals, Jane and John, living in vastly different economic circumstances. Jane, a high-powered executive with a six-figure salary, designer wardrobe, and a penthouse view. John, a schoolteacher with a modest income, living in a small suburban home. Who do you think is happier? The answer might surprise you.

In this chapter, we'll explore how economic factors like income, wealth, employment, and economic stability influence our happiness. We'll debunk myths, examine surprising research findings, and uncover the nuanced relationship between money and contentment. But we won't stop there. We'll also investigate how societal economic conditions, from inequality to economic growth, shape our collective sense of well-being.

As we navigate through this exploration, two main factors will serve as our compass: the objective measures of economic well-being and the subjective experience of happiness. These twin pillars will guide our understanding of how financial circumstances intersect with our emotional lives.

So, are you ready to crack the code of the happiness equation? Let's embark on this enlightening journey to discover how money matters—and how it doesn't—in our quest for a fulfilling life. By the end of this chapter, you'll have a fresh perspective on the role of economics in the pursuit of happiness, equipped with insights that could reshape your approach to both your finances and your well-being.

Fasten your seatbelts, we're about to take off on an exhilarating exploration of the intricate dance between dollars and delight!

5.1: How Recessions Affect the Money-Happiness Relationship

Recessions, those periods of economic downturn characterized by declining GDP, rising unemployment, and financial uncertainty, can profoundly impact the delicate balance between money and happiness. To understand this complex relationship, let's explore how recessions influence both our objective financial circumstances and our subjective well-being.

Consider the story of Maria, a marketing executive, and Tom, a freelance graphic designer, during the 2008 financial crisis:

Maria's Experience:
Before the recession, Maria enjoyed a six-figure salary and felt secure in her position. When the crisis hit, her company downsized, and she faced a 20% pay cut. Initially devastated, Maria found herself reevaluating her priorities and discovering joy in simpler, less expensive activities.

Tom's Experience:
As a freelancer, Tom's income was already variable. When the recession struck, his client base shrunk dramatically. The financial stress took a toll on his mental health, but it also pushed him to diversify his skills and build a more resilient business model.

These personal stories highlight the two main factors at play during recessions:

1. Objective Economic Impact: Reduced income, job loss, and financial instability.

2. Subjective Well-being: Changes in life satisfaction, stress levels, and personal values.

Let's delve deeper into how recessions affect the money-happiness equation:

1. Income Reduction and Job Insecurity:

During recessions, many people face pay cuts, reduced hours, or job loss. This direct hit to income can lead to financial stress and anxiety. However, research shows that the fear of job loss often has a more significant negative impact on happiness than actual income reduction.

2. Shift in Spending Habits:

Economic downturns often force individuals to reassess their spending. While this can be stressful, it can also lead to more mindful consumption and a focus on experiences rather than material goods, potentially enhancing long-term happiness.

3. Social Comparison:

Recessions can reduce the gap between social classes, as even high-earners face financial challenges. This narrowing of inequality can, paradoxically, increase overall societal happiness by reducing the negative effects of social comparison.

4. Resilience and Adaptability:

Surviving a recession can build resilience and adaptability. Many people, like Tom in our example, develop new skills or business models, leading to increased self-efficacy and confidence.

5. Community Bonding:

Economic hardships frequently bring communities closer together. Mutual support systems and shared experiences can enhance social connections, a key factor in happiness.

6. Value Reassessment:

Recessions often trigger a reevaluation of personal values. Many people, like Maria, discover that their pre-recession lifestyle didn't necessarily correlate with higher happiness levels.

7. Financial Literacy:

Economic downturns can motivate individuals to improve their financial literacy. This increased knowledge and control over personal finances can lead to greater financial well-being in the long run.

8. Gratitude and Perspective:

Experiencing financial hardship can foster gratitude for what one has, leading to increased life satisfaction once the economic situation improves.

However, it's crucial to note that the impact of recessions on happiness isn't uniform. Factors such as pre-recession financial stability, social support systems, and individual resilience play significant roles in determining outcomes.

Research by Deaton (2012) found that while life evaluation (a measure of overall life satisfaction) declined during the Great Recession, daily emotional well-being did not show the same drop. This suggests that people's day-to-day emotional experiences may be more resilient to economic shocks than their overall life assessments.

To help navigate the money-happiness relationship during economic downturns, consider these actionable tips:

1. Financial Stress Audit: List your financial stressors. Next to each, write down one action you can take to address or mitigate it.

2. Gratitude Practice: Each day, write down three things you're grateful for that don't cost money. This helps shift focus from financial concerns to life's free joys.

3. Skill Development Plan: Identify one skill you could develop that would make you more resilient in your career. Create a plan to acquire or improve this skill.

4. Budget Reassessment: Review your expenses and identify items that don't significantly contribute to your happiness. Consider eliminating or reducing these to build financial resilience.

5. Community Connection: Find one way to connect with or contribute to your community this week, such as volunteering or joining a local group.

By engaging in these exercises, you can work on both the objective (financial stability) and subjective (emotional well-being) aspects of the money-happiness equation during challenging economic times.

To wrap up, while recessions undoubtedly pose significant challenges to both our finances and our happiness, they also present opportunities for growth, resilience, and a reassessment of what truly matters in life. By understanding the complex interplay between economic factors and well-being, we can navigate these turbulent times with greater emotional balance and financial wisdom.

5.2: Inflation and its Psychological Impact on Well-being

Inflation, the steady increase in the price of goods and services over time, is more than just an economic phenomenon. It's a force that can significantly impact our psychological well-being and financial decision-making. To understand this complex relationship, let's explore how inflation affects both our objective financial circumstances and our subjective perception of economic stability.

Consider the experiences of two individuals: Sarah, a retiree living on a fixed income, and Alex, a young professional in a growing tech industry.

Sarah's Story:
Sarah had carefully planned her retirement, believing her savings would comfortably cover her expenses. However, as inflation rates climbed, she found her purchasing power steadily eroding. The stress of stretching her fixed income to meet rising costs began to take a toll on her peace of mind.

Alex's Experience:
While Alex's salary increased annually, he noticed that his raises barely kept pace with inflation. Despite earning more each year, he didn't feel any more financially secure. This disparity between his expectations and reality led to frustration and anxiety about his financial future.

These personal anecdotes highlight the two main factors at play when considering inflation's impact on well-being:

1. **Objective Financial Impact:** The actual erosion of purchasing power and changes in financial behavior.
2. **Subjective Psychological Impact:** The stress, anxiety, and changes in perception caused by inflation.

Let's delve deeper into how inflation affects our financial and psychological well-being:

1. **Erosion of Purchasing Power:**

As prices increase, the purchasing power of money diminishes. This can lead to a feeling of financial loss, even when income remains stable. For those on fixed incomes, like Sarah, this effect can be particularly distressing.

2. Uncertainty and Anxiety:

Inflation introduces an element of unpredictability into financial planning. The difficulty in predicting future costs can lead to anxiety about long-term financial security, as Alex experienced.

3. Changed Spending Patterns:

High inflation often leads to changes in consumer behavior. People may rush to buy goods before prices increase further, leading to a sense of urgency and potential overspending.

4. Savings Dilemma:

Inflation can discourage saving, as the value of money held in low-interest accounts decreases over time. This can create a conflict between the desire for financial security and the fear of losing value, leading to stress and indecision.

5. Wage-Price Spiral Perception:

In inflationary periods, people typically expect regular wage increases to keep up with rising prices. When these expectations aren't met, as in Alex's case, it can lead to job dissatisfaction and decreased motivation.

6. Relative Deprivation:

Even if one's absolute standard of living remains the same or improves slightly, the perception that others are getting ahead faster can lead to feelings of relative deprivation and decreased life satisfaction.

7. Loss Aversion:

The psychological principle of loss aversion suggests that people feel the pain of losing money more acutely than the pleasure of gaining it.

Inflation can trigger this response, making people feel like they're constantly losing ground financially.

8. Intergenerational Tensions:
Different age groups may experience inflation's impacts differently, potentially leading to intergenerational conflicts and misunderstandings about financial struggles.

Research by Shiller (1997) found that inflation is one of the most important national concerns for the public, often ranking above other economic issues. This highlights the significant psychological impact inflation can have on a population's well-being.

To help navigate the psychological challenges posed by inflation, consider these actionable tips:

1. Inflation Awareness Journal: For one month, note down instances where you notice price increases. Reflect on your emotional reactions to these changes.

2. Future-Proofing Exercise: List your major expenses and brainstorm ways to reduce or hedge against future price increases for each.

3. Positive Financial Habit Formation: Identify one inflation-fighting financial habit (e.g., regular investment in index funds) and create a plan to incorporate it into your routine.

4. Mindfulness Practice: When feeling anxious about inflation, practice a 5-minute mindfulness exercise to center yourself and reduce stress.

5. Financial Education: Commit to learning one new concept about inflation or personal finance each week. Knowledge can help reduce anxiety and improve decision-making.

By engaging in these exercises, you can work on both the objective (financial preparation) and subjective (emotional resilience) aspects of dealing with inflation.

To sum up, while inflation poses significant challenges to both our finances and our psychological well-being, understanding its impacts can help us develop strategies to mitigate its negative effects. By cultivating awareness, building financial resilience, and managing our emotional responses, we can navigate inflationary periods with greater confidence and maintain our sense of financial well-being.

5.3: Income Inequality and Its Effect on Societal Happiness

Income inequality, the uneven distribution of income across a population, is more than just an economic issue—it's a phenomenon that can profoundly impact the collective well-being of a society. To understand this complex relationship, we need to examine both the objective economic realities and the subjective perceptions that shape societal happiness.

Let's consider the tale of two neighborhoods in the same city: Hillcrest and Valley view.

Hillcrest:

In this affluent area, residents enjoy high-end amenities, excellent schools, and top-notch healthcare. Mark, a successful entrepreneur, lives here. He's financially secure, but often feels disconnected from the broader community and worries about the safety of his wealth.

Valley view:
This working-class neighborhood struggles with underfunded schools and limited access to healthcare. Elena, a skilled worker, resides here. Despite working full-time, she struggles to make ends meet and feels increasingly frustrated by the lack of opportunities for advancement.

These contrasting scenarios highlight the two main factors at play when considering income inequality's impact on societal happiness:

1. Objective Economic Impact: The tangible effects of uneven resource distribution on living standards and opportunities.
2. Subjective Psychological Impact: The perceptions, emotions, and social dynamics influenced by awareness of inequality.

Let's delve deeper into how income inequality affects societal happiness:

1. Social Cohesion:
High levels of inequality can erode social trust and cohesion. When the gap between the rich and poor widens, it becomes harder for people from different economic backgrounds to relate to one another, potentially leading to social fragmentation and reduced overall happiness.

2. Perception of Fairness:
Societies with high inequality often struggle with perceptions of unfairness. When people believe that the economic system is rigged against them, it can lead to widespread dissatisfaction and reduced faith in institutions.

3. Relative Deprivation:
Even as absolute living standards rise, high inequality can make people feel worse off if they perceive others are advancing more rapidly. This psychological phenomenon, known as relative deprivation, can significantly impact happiness levels across society.

4. Health and Well-being:

Research has shown that more unequal societies tend to have poorer health outcomes across all income levels. This includes higher rates of mental health issues, which directly impact societal happiness.

5. Social Mobility:

High inequality often correlates with reduced social mobility. When people perceive limited opportunities to improve their economic situation, it can lead to feelings of hopelessness and reduced overall life satisfaction.

6. Political Polarization:

Income inequality can fuel political divisions, as different segments of society advocate for policies that align with their economic interests. This polarization can create a tense social atmosphere that negatively impacts collective well-being.

7. Crime and Safety:

Societies with high inequality often experience higher crime rates, which can lead to increased fear and reduced quality of life for all members of society, regardless of their income level.

8. Education and Opportunity:

Unequal access to quality education perpetuates income inequality across generations. This can lead to a sense of injustice and frustration, particularly among those with limited access to educational opportunities.

A study by Oishi, Kesebir, and Diener (2011) found that Americans were happier in years when national income inequality was lower. The researchers attributed this to a greater sense of fairness and trust in others during periods of lower inequality.

To help navigate the challenges posed by income inequality and contribute to a happier society, consider these actionable tips:

1. Empathy Building: Spend a day volunteering in a community different from your own. Reflect on the experience and how it changes your perspective on inequality.

2. Civic Engagement: Identify one local issue related to inequality (e.g., education funding) and find a way to get involved, such as attending a town hall meeting or joining a community group.

3. Skill Sharing: Offer to teach a skill you have to someone who might not have had the same opportunities. This could be through formal mentoring or informal community interactions.

4. Conscious Consumption: Research the labor practices of companies you frequently buy from. Make an effort to support businesses that prioritize fair wages and working conditions.

5. Gratitude and Perspective: Keep a gratitude journal, but also regularly acknowledge the systemic advantages or challenges you may have faced due to your economic position.

By engaging in these exercises, you can work on both the objective (community involvement) and subjective (empathy and awareness) aspects of addressing income inequality's impact on societal happiness.

To wrap up, while income inequality poses significant challenges to societal well-being, understanding its impacts can help us develop strategies to mitigate its negative effects. By fostering empathy, engaging in our communities, and working towards more equitable systems, we can contribute to building a society where happiness is more evenly distributed along with economic resources.

5.4: Case Study: Comparing Happiness Levels in Countries with Different Economic Systems

To truly understand the relationship between economic systems and happiness, let's embark on a comparative journey across three nations with distinct economic models: the United States, Sweden, and Singapore. Each of these countries represents a different approach to balancing free market principles with government intervention, providing us with a rich tapestry of data to explore.

As we delve into this case study, we'll focus on two main factors:

1. **Objective Economic Indicators:** GDP per capita, income distribution, social safety nets, and economic opportunities.
2. **Subjective Well-being Measures:** Self-reported happiness levels, life satisfaction, and social trust.

Let's examine each country in turn:

United States: Capitalist Free Market Economy

The United States is often seen as the epitome of a capitalist free market economy. It boasts:

- High GDP per capita ($63,544 in 2020)
- Strong emphasis on individual economic freedom
- Relatively low taxes and limited government intervention

However, it also faces challenges:

- High income inequality (Gini coefficient of 0.41 in 2018)
- Limited social safety nets compared to other developed nations

Sarah, a software engineer in Silicon Valley, represents the American dream. She enjoys a high salary and numerous career opportunities. However, she also faces high stress levels due to job insecurity and expensive healthcare costs.

Happiness score (World Happiness Report 2021): 6.951 out of 10

Sweden: Social Democratic Welfare State

Sweden represents the Nordic model of a social democratic welfare state, characterized by:

- High taxes funding extensive social services
- Strong labor unions and worker protections
- Relatively low income inequality (Gini coefficient of 0.27 in 2018)

Anders, a middle-class worker in Stockholm, benefits from free education, universal healthcare, and generous parental leave. While his take-home pay is lower due to high taxes, he feels secure and reports high life satisfaction.

Happiness score (World Happiness Report 2021): 7.363 out of 10

Singapore: Managed Capitalist Economy

Singapore presents a unique model of a managed capitalist economy, featuring:

- Low taxes and business-friendly policies
- Strong government intervention in key sectors like housing and healthcare
- High GDP per capita ($59,798 in 2020)

Mei Ling, a young professional in Singapore, appreciates the country's efficiency and economic opportunities. She benefits from subsidized housing and healthcare, but sometimes feels stressed by the competitive work culture.

Happiness score (World Happiness Report 2021): 6.377 out of 10

Comparative Analysis:

1. Economic Security vs. Opportunity:
Sweden's model provides the highest level of economic security, which translates into high happiness scores. The US offers more economic opportunities but with less security, leading to mixed outcomes for happiness. Singapore balances both, resulting in moderate happiness levels.

2. Income Inequality:
Sweden's low-income inequality correlates with higher happiness levels, supporting the idea that relative income matters for well-being. The US, with high inequality, scores lower on happiness despite higher absolute incomes.

3. Social Trust:
Sweden's high social trust, partly attributed to its universal welfare system, contributes to its high happiness score. The US and Singapore, with more individualistic cultures, score lower on social trust metrics.

4. Work-Life Balance:
Sweden's emphasis on work-life balance (e.g., generous vacation time) seems to boost happiness. The US and Singapore, known for longer working hours, may see happiness levels impacted as a result.

5. Healthcare and Education:

Universal access to healthcare and education in Sweden reduces stress and contributes to higher life satisfaction. The US's private system creates anxiety for many, potentially lowering overall happiness.

This case study reveals that while economic prosperity is important, the structure of the economic system and how it addresses issues like inequality, social security, and work-life balance play crucial roles in determining societal happiness.

Actionable Tips:

1. Personal Economic System Audit: Reflect on which aspects of each country's system resonate with you. How could you incorporate these principles into your personal financial philosophy?

2. Community Building: Inspired by Sweden's high social trust, identify one way to build stronger connections in your community this month.

3. Work-Life Balance Challenge: Try adopting a Swedish-inspired approach to work-life balance for a week. How does it affect your happiness?

4. Security vs. Opportunity Reflection: Consider your current balance of economic security and opportunity. Write down one step you could take to improve this balance.

5. Global Perspective Exercise: Research happiness levels in a country with a different economic system than your own. What lessons could you apply to your life?

By engaging with these exercises, you can gain insights from different economic systems and apply them to enhance your personal happiness and financial well-being.

To sum up, this case study illustrates that there's no one-size-fits-all economic system for maximizing happiness. Each model has its strengths and weaknesses. By understanding these differences, we can work towards creating economic systems and personal financial strategies that better support overall well-being.

Chapter 6: Money and Happiness Across the Lifespan

From piggy banks to pension plans, our relationship with money evolves as we journey through life. But does our happiness follow the same trajectory? In this chapter, we'll explore the fascinating interplay between financial well-being and personal contentment as we age.

Picture a winding road that stretches from childhood to retirement. Along this path, we encounter various financial milestones and challenges. At each turn, we'll examine how our attitudes towards money shift and how these changes impact our overall sense of happiness.

Two main factors shape this lifelong journey:

1. Financial Circumstances: The objective reality of our economic situation at different life stages.

2. Psychological Perceptions: Our subjective understanding and emotional responses to money matters as we mature.

As we navigate through this chapter, we'll uncover surprising insights about how financial priorities and sources of happiness transform over time. We'll debunk common myths, such as the belief that more money always leads to greater happiness, and reveal how age-specific financial concerns can influence our well-being.

Get ready to embark on a voyage of discovery that spans generations. We'll explore how a child's joy over a few coins in a piggy bank evolves into a teenager's first taste of financial independence, an adult's complex financial responsibilities, and a retiree's reflection on a lifetime of economic decisions.

By understanding these patterns, you'll gain valuable insights into managing your own financial journey for maximum happiness. Whether you're just starting out or looking back on years of financial experiences, this chapter offers a fresh perspective on the age-old question: Can money buy happiness?

Let's set off on this illuminating expedition through the various stages of life, where dollars and joy intersect in unexpected ways.

6.1: Childhood: How Early Experiences Shape Money Attitudes

Our relationship with money begins long before we earn our first paycheck or open a bank account. The foundations of our financial attitudes are laid in childhood, shaped by the experiences and observations we encounter during our formative years. This subchapter explores how these early influences mold our perceptions of money and its connection to happiness.

To understand this crucial phase, we'll focus on two main factors:

1. **Environmental Influences:** The external circumstances and examples that children observe.
2. **Personal Experiences:** The direct interactions children have with money.

Let's delve into how these factors play out in real-life scenarios:

The Allowance Experiment:

Consider two siblings, Emma and Jack, raised in the same household but with different approaches to pocket money.

Emma receives a fixed weekly allowance, regardless of her behavior or chores completed. This teaches her to budget and plan, but she may not associate money with effort or achievement.

Jack, on the other hand, earns his allowance through completing tasks around the house. This instills in him a strong work ethic and the concept that money is a reward for effort.

These contrasting approaches can lead to very different money attitudes in adulthood. Emma might become a careful planner, while Jack could develop a strong drive to earn and achieve financially.

The Impact of Parental Attitudes:

Children are keen observers, absorbing their parents' attitudes towards money like sponges. Let's look at how this plays out in the Thompson family:

Mr. Thompson frequently expresses anxiety about bills and financial struggles, often saying, "We can't afford that." This constant stress around money may instill a scarcity mindset in his children.

Mrs. Thompson, while equally conscious of their financial limitations, approaches the subject differently. She involves the children in budgeting discussions, teaching them about prioritizing expenses and saving for goals. This approach fosters a more positive and empowering relationship with money.

As a result, the Thompson children might develop different attitudes:
- One child might become overly cautious with spending, always fearing financial instability.
- Another might adopt a more balanced approach, seeing money as a tool to be managed rather than a source of anxiety.

The Role of Socioeconomic Background:
A child's socioeconomic environment plays a crucial role in shaping their money attitudes. Consider the contrasting experiences of Zoe and Miguel:

Zoe grows up in an affluent neighborhood. She's accustomed to seeing material wealth and may associate happiness with having expensive possessions. However, she might also take financial security for granted.

Miguel comes from a working-class family. He witnesses his parents' hard work and careful budgeting. This could instill in him a strong value for money and a drive for financial security, but it might also lead to anxiety around financial matters.

These early experiences can have lasting impacts on how Zoe and Miguel perceive the relationship between money and happiness in adulthood.

The Power of Financial Education:

Early financial education can significantly influence a child's future relationship with money. Schools that incorporate financial literacy into their curriculum give students a head start in understanding money management.

For instance, a study by the University of Cambridge found that money habits are formed by age seven. This underscores the importance of early financial education, both at home and in schools.

As we transition from childhood to adolescence, these early experiences and lessons form the bedrock of our financial attitudes. They shape our beliefs about whether money can buy happiness, how much is "enough," and what role financial success should play in our lives.

Actionable Tips for Parents and Caregivers:

1. Money Conversation Starter: Choose one day a week to have an age-appropriate discussion about a financial topic with your child. This could range from explaining what money is to younger children, to discussing budgeting with teenagers.

2. Allowance Reflection: If you give your child an allowance, reflect on the system you use. Consider trying a different approach for a month and observe how it affects your child's attitude towards money.

3. Values Clarification Exercise: Make a list of the top five money values you want to instill in your child (e.g., generosity, saving, hard work). Brainstorm specific ways to demonstrate these values in your daily life.

4. Financial Literacy Game Night: Once a month, play a board game that teaches financial concepts, like Monopoly or The Game of Life. Use it as an opportunity to discuss real-world financial scenarios.

5. Giving Project: Involve your child in choosing and supporting a charitable cause. This can help develop a sense of perspective about money and its ability to effect positive change.

By implementing these exercises, parents, and caregivers can play an active role in shaping positive money attitudes in children, setting the stage for a healthier relationship with finances in adulthood.

To wrap up, the financial attitudes formed in childhood have a profound and lasting impact on our relationship with money throughout our lives. By understanding these early influences, we can better comprehend our own money behaviors and work towards fostering positive financial mindsets in the next generation.

6.2: Young Adulthood: Financial Stress vs. Opportunity

As we transition from childhood to young adulthood, our relationship with money undergoes a significant transformation. This period, typically spanning from late teens to early thirties, is characterized by a unique juxtaposition of financial stress and unprecedented opportunities. To understand this complex phase, we'll explore two main factors:

1. Economic Challenges: The financial hurdles and responsibilities young adults face.

2. Growth Potential: The opportunities for financial advancement and personal development.

Let's dive into how these factors play out in real-life scenarios:

The Student Debt Dilemma:

Meet Alex, a 23-year-old recent college graduate. Like many of her peers, Alex is grappling with substantial student loan debt. This financial burden colors her perception of money and happiness:

On one hand, Alex feels stressed about her monthly loan payments and how they limit her current lifestyle choices. She often has to decline social invitations, leading to feelings of isolation and frustration.

On the other hand, her education has opened doors to career opportunities that were previously unavailable. Alex landed a job in her chosen field, which gives her a sense of accomplishment and hope for future financial stability.

This duality of stress and opportunity is a common experience for many young adults navigating student debt.

The Gig Economy Adventure:

Now, let's consider the case of Marcus, a 28-year-old freelance graphic designer. Marcus represents a growing trend among young adults who are embracing the gig economy:

The flexibility of freelance work allows Marcus to pursue his passions and maintain a work-life balance that contributes to his overall happiness. He enjoys the freedom to choose his projects and set his own schedule.

However, the inconsistent income and lack of traditional benefits like health insurance and retirement plans create financial anxiety. Marcus often worries about saving for the future and handling unexpected expenses.

This scenario illustrates how the changing nature of work in young adulthood can simultaneously offer exciting opportunities and introduce new financial stressors.

The Housing Market Challenge:

Emma and James, both 30, are navigating the complex world of homeownership. Their experience highlights a common financial milestone for young adults:

The couple feels pressure to buy a home, seeing it as a step towards financial stability and adulthood. They're excited about the prospect of building equity and creating a space of their own.

Yet, rising housing costs in their area make this goal seem increasingly unattainable. They're torn between stretching their finances to buy now or continuing to rent while saving for a larger down payment.

This situation demonstrates how traditional markers of financial success can become sources of stress and uncertainty for young adults.

Career Growth vs. Financial Stability:

Let's examine the story of Raj, a 26-year-old software engineer facing a career crossroads:

Raj has received a job offer from a promising startup. The position offers stock options and the potential for significant financial gain if the company succeeds. It aligns with his passion for innovative technology and could accelerate his career growth.

However, accepting this offer would mean leaving his stable, well-paying job at an established company. Raj is torn between the excitement of potential rewards and the security of his current position.

This dilemma encapsulates the balance many young adults must strike between pursuing opportunities for growth and maintaining financial stability.

As we navigate through young adulthood, these experiences shape our evolving relationship with money and its impact on our happiness. The financial decisions made during this period often have long-lasting effects, influencing our financial well-being and life satisfaction for years to come.

Actionable Tips for Young Adults:

1. Financial Goal Setting Exercise: Write down three short-term (1 year) and three long-term (5+ years) financial goals. Break each goal into smaller, actionable steps and create a timeline for achieving them.

2. Stress vs. Opportunity Journal: For one week, keep a daily log of your financial stressors and opportunities. At the end of the week, reflect on patterns and brainstorm ways to minimize stress and maximize opportunities.

3. Skill Investment Challenge: Identify one skill that could increase your earning potential. Commit to spending 30 minutes a day for a month learning or improving this skill.

4. Budget Reallocation Experiment: Review your current budget and identify one area where you can cut back. Reallocate that money to either debt repayment, savings, or personal development. Track how this change affects your financial stress and overall happiness.

5. Financial Mentor Connection: Reach out to someone you admire for their financial acumen. Ask if they'd be willing to have a coffee (virtual or in-person) to discuss their experiences navigating finances in young adulthood.

By engaging with these exercises, young adults can proactively manage the balance between financial stress and opportunity, potentially leading to greater financial well-being and life satisfaction.

To sum up, young adulthood is a period of financial contrasts. While it comes with its share of economic challenges, it also presents unique opportunities for growth and development. By understanding and navigating this duality, young adults can lay the groundwork for a healthier, happier relationship with money as they progress through life.

6.3: Middle Age: Balancing Financial Responsibilities and Personal Fulfillment

As we enter middle age, typically spanning from our late 30s to early 60s, our relationship with money evolves yet again. This stage of life often brings peak earning potential, but also heightened financial responsibilities. The challenge lies in striking a balance between meeting these obligations and pursuing personal fulfillment. To understand this complex phase, we'll explore two main factors:

1. Financial Obligations: The increasing financial responsibilities that come with middle age.
2. Personal Aspirations: The desire for self-actualization and life satisfaction.

Let's examine how these factors play out in real-life scenarios:

The Sandwich Generation Squeeze:

Meet Linda, a 45-year-old marketing executive. Linda exemplifies the "sandwich generation," simultaneously supporting her teenage children and her aging parents:

Financial Obligations:
Linda juggles mortgage payments, her children's education costs, and contributing to her parents' healthcare expenses. These responsibilities frequently leave her feeling financially stretched and stressed.

Personal Aspirations:
Despite her busy schedule, Linda dreams of starting her own business. She's passionate about sustainable fashion but struggles to find the time and resources to pursue this goal.

Linda's situation highlights the common middle-age dilemma of balancing family obligations with personal dreams. Her financial decisions directly impact not just her own happiness, but the well-being of two other generations.

The Mid-Career Crossroads:

Consider the case of Robert, a 52-year-old accountant contemplating a major career shift:

Financial Obligations:
Robert has a stable, well-paying job that allows him to support his family comfortably. He's on track with his retirement savings and has built a solid financial foundation.

Personal Aspirations:
Despite his financial success, Robert feels unfulfilled in his career. He's considering leaving accounting to become a high school teacher, a long-held dream that aligns more closely with his values.

Robert's dilemma illustrates the tension many middle-aged adults face between maintaining financial security and pursuing more personally rewarding paths.

The Empty Nest Financial Shift:

Let's look at Maria and John, both 55, whose children have recently left for college:

Financial Obligations:
The couple is adjusting to new financial dynamics. While they no longer have daily expenses for their children at home, they're now managing college tuition payments and trying to boost their retirement savings.

Personal Aspirations:
With an empty nest, Maria and John are excited about the opportunity to travel and pursue hobbies they've put off for years. However, they're unsure how to balance these desires with their financial responsibilities.

This scenario demonstrates how life transitions in middle age can prompt a reevaluation of financial priorities and personal goals.

The Entrepreneurial Leap:

Meet Samantha, a 48-year-old who recently launched her own consulting firm:

Financial Obligations:

Samantha took a significant financial risk by leaving her corporate job. She's navigating the uncertainties of entrepreneurship while maintaining her family's financial stability.

Personal Aspirations:
Starting her own business has been a long-held dream for Samantha. The autonomy and potential for growth bring her a sense of fulfillment she hadn't experienced in her previous role.

Samantha's story showcases how middle age can be a time of bold moves towards personal fulfillment, even as financial responsibilities remain significant.

As we navigate through middle age, these experiences shape our evolving perspective on the relationship between money and happiness. The financial decisions made during this period often require careful balancing of immediate responsibilities with long-term personal and financial goals.

Actionable Tips for Middle-Aged Adults:

1. Values and Goals Alignment Exercise: List your top five personal values and your top five financial goals. Identify areas of alignment and conflict. Brainstorm ways to bring your financial decisions more in line with your personal values.

2. Financial Responsibility Audit: Create a comprehensive list of your current financial obligations. Categorize them as "essential," "important," and "optional." Look for areas where you might be able to reduce commitments without significantly impacting your or your family's well-being.

3. Personal Fulfillment Fund: Set up a separate savings account dedicated to personal aspirations. Commit to putting a small percentage of your income into this fund each month, treating it with the same importance as your other financial obligations.

4. Skills and Passions Inventory: Make a list of your skills, experiences, and passions. Explore ways to monetize these in your current career or as a side hustle, potentially creating new streams of income that align with your interests.

5. Financial What-If Scenarios: Model out the financial implications of major life changes you're considering (career shift, starting a business, etc.). Create best-case, worst-case, and most-likely scenarios to help you make informed decisions.

By engaging with these exercises, middle-aged adults can work towards finding a balance between meeting their financial responsibilities and pursuing personal fulfillment. This balance is key to maintaining both financial stability and life satisfaction during this dynamic phase of life.

To wrap up, middle age presents a unique set of financial challenges and opportunities. While financial responsibilities often peak during this time, it's also a period ripe for personal growth and self-actualization. By thoughtfully balancing obligations with aspirations, individuals can navigate this stage of life in a way that promotes both financial security and personal happiness.

6.4: Retirement: The Role of Financial Security in Late-Life Satisfaction

As we enter the retirement phase of life, typically beginning in our 60s or 70s, our relationship with money undergoes yet another significant transformation. This stage marks a shift from active income generation to relying on accumulated savings and investments. The interplay between financial security and life satisfaction becomes more pronounced than ever before. To understand this crucial phase, we'll explore two main factors:

1. Financial Preparedness: The level of financial readiness for retirement.
2. Quality of Life: How financial resources contribute to overall well-being in retirement.

Let's examine how these factors manifest in real-life scenarios:

The Well-Prepared Retiree:

Meet Eleanor, a 68-year-old former teacher who planned meticulously for her retirement:

Financial Preparedness:
Eleanor started saving early in her career and maximized her pension contributions. She also invested wisely in a diversified portfolio. As a result, she entered retirement with a comfortable nest egg.

Quality of Life:
Eleanor's financial security allows her to pursue her passions without constant worry about money. She travels regularly, takes art classes, and contributes to causes she cares about. Her financial stability contributes significantly to her sense of freedom and overall life satisfaction.

Eleanor's case illustrates how thorough financial preparation can lead to a fulfilling retirement, where money serves as a tool for enhancing life experiences rather than a source of stress.

The Late Starter:

Consider the situation of Frank, a 72-year-old who didn't prioritize retirement savings until later in life:

Financial Preparedness:
Frank focused on immediate financial needs throughout his career, putting off retirement planning. He now relies heavily on Social Security and a modest savings account, which limits his financial flexibility.

Quality of Life:
While Frank enjoys aspects of retirement, such as spending time with family, he often feels constrained by his financial situation. He's unable to pursue some of his retirement dreams, like extensive travel, and worries about potential healthcare costs.

Frank's experience highlights how insufficient financial preparation can impact retirement satisfaction, underscoring the importance of early and consistent retirement planning.

The Entrepreneurial Retiree:

Let's look at the case of Martha, a 65-year-old who views retirement as a new beginning:

Financial Preparedness:
Martha has a solid retirement fund from her corporate career. However, instead of fully retiring, she decided to start a small online business based on her hobby of crafting.

Quality of Life:
The additional income from her business allows Martha to splurge on extras without dipping into her retirement savings. Moreover, the mental stimulation and sense of purpose she derives from her business contribute significantly to her happiness and vitality in retirement.

Martha's story demonstrates how retirement can be an opportunity for new ventures that enhance both financial security and personal fulfillment.

The Health-Challenged Retiree:

Consider the situation of George, a 70-year-old facing significant health issues:

Financial Preparedness:
George saved diligently for retirement, but underestimated his healthcare costs. His chronic health condition requires expensive treatments not fully covered by insurance.

Quality of Life:
While George's savings provide a buffer, the ongoing medical expenses create financial stress. This situation highlights how health can be a wild card in retirement planning, potentially impacting both financial security and life satisfaction.

George's case underscores the importance of factoring in potential health costs when planning for retirement.

As we navigate through retirement, these experiences shape our understanding of how financial security contributes to late-life satisfaction. The financial decisions made throughout our lives culminate in this stage, significantly influencing our ability to enjoy our golden years.

Actionable Tips for Retirees and Pre-Retirees:

1. Retirement Lifestyle Budgeting Exercise: Create two budgets - one for your "basic" retirement lifestyle and another for your "ideal" retirement lifestyle. Compare these to your projected retirement income to identify any gaps and adjust your savings or expectations accordingly.

2. Health Cost Projection: Research the average healthcare costs for retirees in your area. Create a separate savings fund specifically for potential medical expenses not covered by insurance or Medicare.

3. Purpose Planning Workshop: Spend a week noting down activities that give you a sense of purpose or joy. Use this list to plan how you'll spend your time in retirement and consider if any of these activities could generate supplemental income.

4. Social Security Strategy Review: If you're nearing retirement, review your Social Security claiming options. Consider consulting with a financial advisor to determine the optimal time to start receiving benefits based on your unique situation.

5. Legacy and Giving Plan: Reflect on what you'd like your financial legacy to be. Create a plan for charitable giving or family inheritances that aligns with your values and financial capacity.

By engaging with these exercises, both retirees and those approaching retirement can work towards aligning their financial resources with their desired quality of life. This alignment is crucial for maximizing satisfaction and minimizing stress during the retirement years.

To sum up, financial security plays a pivotal role in shaping late-life satisfaction. While money alone doesn't guarantee happiness in retirement, it provides the freedom to pursue fulfilling activities, manage health challenges, and maintain peace of mind. By understanding this relationship and planning accordingly, individuals can set the stage for a more satisfying and enjoyable retirement experience.

6.5: Case Studies: Individuals at Different Life Stages and Their Relationship with Money

In this subchapter, we'll explore real-life examples of individuals at various life stages and examine how their relationship with money impacts their overall happiness and well-being. Through these case studies, we'll analyze two main factors:

1. Financial Behaviors: The actions and decisions individuals make regarding money.

2. Emotional Responses: How these financial behaviors affect their emotional state and life satisfaction.

Let's dive into these illuminating stories:

The Recent Graduate: Sarah, 23

Financial Behaviors:
Sarah recently graduated with a degree in engineering and landed her first job. She's excited about her new income but feels overwhelmed by student loan debt. Sarah has started budgeting for the first time and is trying to balance loan repayments with building an emergency fund.

Emotional Responses:
While Sarah feels proud of her accomplishments, she often experiences anxiety about her financial future. The weight of her student loans sometimes makes her question the value of her education. However, she finds satisfaction in taking control of her finances through budgeting and planning.

Lesson: For young adults like Sarah, developing financial literacy and creating a structured approach to managing money can help alleviate anxiety and build confidence.

The Young Family: The Patel Family (Raj, 32, and Priya, 30)
Financial Behaviors:
Raj and Priya are juggling multiple financial priorities. They're saving for a down payment on a house, while also starting to invest in their children's education funds. Raj recently started a side hustle to supplement their income.

Emotional Responses:
The couple feels stretched thin financially and sometimes argues about money. However, they also experience a sense of accomplishment as they make progress towards their goals. Raj's side hustle brings him additional stress but also a feeling of security.

Lesson: For young families, open communication about financial goals and shared decision-making can help maintain harmony and reduce money-related stress.

The Mid-Career Professional: Michael, 45

Financial Behaviors:
Michael is at the peak of his earning potential in his corporate job. He's maxing out his retirement contributions and has a solid investment portfolio. However, he's considering taking a pay cut to switch to a less stressful, more fulfilling career.

Emotional Responses:
While Michael feels financially secure, he's increasingly dissatisfied with his work. He worries about the potential impact of a career change on his family's lifestyle but is also excited about the possibility of pursuing more meaningful work.

Lesson: For mid-career professionals like Michael, balancing financial security with personal fulfillment becomes crucial for overall life satisfaction.

The Empty Nesters: Linda and Tom, both 58

Financial Behaviors:
With their children now independent, Linda and Tom are reassessing their financial priorities. They're increasing their retirement savings, but also allocating more funds for travel and hobbies. They're debating whether to downsize their home.

Emotional Responses:
The couple feels a mix of excitement and apprehension about this new phase of life. They enjoy the financial freedom that comes with reduced family responsibilities, but sometimes worry if they're saving enough for retirement.

Lesson: For empty nesters, finding a balance between enjoying the present and preparing for the future is key to financial and emotional well-being.

The Retiree: Eleanor, 72

Financial Behaviors:
Eleanor lives on a combination of Social Security, pension, and retirement account withdrawals. She's cautious with her spending to ensure her savings last, but also prioritizes experiences like traveling and taking classes.

Emotional Responses:
Eleanor feels grateful for her financial stability, but occasionally worries about potential health care costs. She finds joy in using her money to create meaningful experiences and help her grandchildren.

Lesson: For retirees like Eleanor, financial security provides a foundation for pursuing personal interests and maintaining peace of mind.

These case studies highlight how our relationship with money evolves throughout different life stages. They demonstrate that financial behaviors and emotional responses are deeply interconnected, influencing our overall happiness and life satisfaction.

Actionable Tips and Exercises:

1. Financial Life Stage Assessment: Identify which case study most closely resembles your current situation. Write down similarities and differences in your financial behaviors and emotional responses.

2. Money Emotion Diary: For one week, keep a daily log of your financial actions and the emotions they evoke. Look for patterns to understand your emotional relationship with money better.

3. Future Self Visualization: Write a letter to your future self, 10 years from now, describing your ideal financial situation and how it contributes to your happiness. Use this as a guide for setting long-term financial goals.

4. Financial Behavior Audit: List your top five financial habits. Rate each on a scale of 1-10 for how well it serves your long-term financial goals and emotional well-being. Identify one habit to improve or replace.

5. Cross-Generational Money Discussion: Have a conversation about money with someone at a different life stage (e.g., a parent, child, or mentor). Share insights about how your perspectives on money and happiness differ or align.

By engaging with these exercises, readers can gain deeper insights into their own financial behaviors and emotional responses, helping them navigate their unique financial journey more effectively.

To wrap up, these case studies illustrate that our relationship with money is not static but evolves as we move through different life stages. By understanding these shifts and actively managing both our financial behaviors and emotional responses, we can work towards a healthier, more balanced relationship with money that supports our overall happiness and well-being.

Chapter 7: Redefining the Good Life

What does it truly mean to live a good life? For generations, society has often equated a life well-lived with financial prosperity and material abundance. However, as we delve deeper into the complexities of human happiness and fulfillment, it becomes clear that the traditional definition of success may be due for a significant overhaul.

In this transformative chapter, we'll embark on a journey to redefine the concept of the "good life" through the lens of two pivotal factors:

1. **Holistic Well-being:** The integration of physical, mental, emotional, and spiritual health.
2. **Sustainable Contentment:** The ability to find lasting satisfaction beyond fleeting pleasures or material gains.

As we navigate through this exploration, we'll challenge long-held beliefs about success and happiness, examining how our perceptions of a fulfilling life have evolved in response to societal changes, technological advancements, and shifting values.

Consider for a moment: How many times have you achieved a financial goal, only to find that the satisfaction was short-lived? Or conversely, when have you experienced profound joy from something that cost little or nothing at all? These experiences hint at a deeper truth about human fulfillment that goes beyond monetary measures.

Throughout this chapter, we'll draw insights from various fields including psychology, philosophy, and social sciences to paint a more comprehensive picture of what truly constitutes a life well-lived. We'll explore how factors such as meaningful relationships, personal growth, community engagement, and a sense of purpose contribute to our overall sense of well-being and contentment.

Moreover, we'll delve into the concept of sustainable contentment, examining how we can cultivate a sense of fulfillment that withstands the test of time and circumstances. This involves developing resilience, practicing gratitude, and aligning our actions with our core values.

By the end of this chapter, you'll have a fresh perspective on what it means to live a good life. You'll be equipped with practical strategies to assess and enhance your own well-being, and you'll understand how to cultivate sustainable contentment in an ever-changing world.

Prepare to challenge your assumptions, broaden your horizons, and embark on a transformative journey towards a more authentic and fulfilling definition of the good life. This exploration promises not just to change how you view success, but how you approach life itself.

7.1: What Really Moves Life's Satisfaction Needle

In our quest to understand what truly enhances life satisfaction, we often find ourselves navigating a complex web of factors. While financial stability plays a role, it's far from the whole story. This subchapter explores the elements that genuinely impact our sense of fulfillment and contentment. We'll focus on two main factors:

1. Intrinsic Motivators: Internal drivers that fuel our sense of purpose and personal growth.
2. Social Connections: The quality and depth of our relationships with others.

Let's delve into these factors and examine how they influence our overall life satisfaction.

Intrinsic Motivators: The Power of Purpose

Meet Sarah, a 35-year-old marketing executive. On paper, Sarah had it all - a six-figure salary, a luxury apartment, and frequent exotic vacations. Yet, she felt unfulfilled. Sarah's story illustrates a common misconception: that external success automatically translates to inner satisfaction.

After much soul-searching, Sarah realized her work lacked personal meaning. She decided to pivot her career, taking a pay cut to join a non-profit organization aligned with her values. Despite the reduced income, Sarah reported a significant boost in her overall life satisfaction.

Sarah's experience highlights the potency of intrinsic motivators. When our actions align with our values and provide a sense of purpose, we're more likely to experience lasting satisfaction. This internal drive often proves more powerful than external rewards in moving the life satisfaction needle.

Social Connections: The Fabric of Fulfillment

Now, consider the case of Tom, a 45-year-old software engineer. Tom earned an impressive salary and lived in a beautiful home. However, his demanding job left little time for socializing or maintaining relationships. Despite his financial success, Tom typically felt lonely and disconnected.

Recognizing this issue, Tom made a conscious effort to nurture his relationships. He joined a local sports club, reconnected with old friends, and prioritized family time. The result? A marked improvement in his overall happiness and life satisfaction.

Tom's story underscores the crucial role of social connections in our well-being. Meaningful relationships provide emotional support, shared experiences, and a sense of belonging - all vital components of life satisfaction that money alone can't buy.

The Interplay of Factors

While we've examined intrinsic motivators and social connections separately, it's important to note that these factors often intertwine and reinforce each other. Let's look at the case of Maria, a 50-year-old teacher, to illustrate this point.

Maria found great purpose in her work, satisfying her need for intrinsic motivation. Her role also allowed her to form strong connections with her students and colleagues, fulfilling her social needs. The combination of these factors resulted in high levels of life satisfaction for Maria, despite a modest income.

Maria's experience demonstrates how intrinsic motivators and social connections can work in tandem to significantly boost overall life satisfaction.

The Role of Financial Stability

It's crucial to acknowledge that financial stability does play a role in life satisfaction. However, research suggests that beyond a certain point - often referred to as the "income satiation point" - additional income has diminishing returns on happiness.

A study by Princeton University researchers found that emotional well-being rises with income, but there's no further progress beyond an annual income of ~$75,000 (adjusted for cost of living). This finding suggests that once our basic needs are met, other factors become more critical in moving the life satisfaction needle.

Actionable Tips and Exercises:

. **Purpose Mapping:** Create a "purpose map" by listing your core values, passions, and skills. Identify areas where these intersect to uncover potential sources of intrinsic motivation.

2. Relationship Audit: Assess the quality of your key relationships. Rate each on a scale of 1-10 for factors like trust, support, and mutual understanding. Identify one action you can take to strengthen each relationship.

3. Gratitude Journal: For one week, write down three things you're grateful for each day. Notice how this practice impacts your overall sense of life satisfaction.

4. Values-Based Decision-Making: Before making your next significant decision, explicitly consider how it aligns with your core values. Does it support your intrinsic motivations?

5. Connection Challenge: Reach out to one person you care about but haven't spoken to recently. Schedule a catch-up call or meeting. Reflect on how this interaction affects your mood and sense of fulfillment.

By engaging with these exercises, you can start to identify and cultivate the factors that truly move your personal life satisfaction needle.

To wrap up, while financial stability provides a foundation, it's the combination of intrinsic motivators and quality social connections that often proves most potent in enhancing life satisfaction. By understanding and nurturing these elements, we can work towards a more fulfilling and contented life, regardless of our income level.

7.2: Savoring Life's Experiences Over Acquisition

In our pursuit of happiness and fulfillment, we often find ourselves at a crossroads: should we invest in experiences or accumulate more possessions? This subchapter explores the profound impact of prioritizing experiences over material acquisitions. We'll examine this concept through two main factors:

1. Psychological Impact: How experiences and possessions differently affect our mental well-being.
2. Long-term Value: The enduring benefits of experiences compared to material goods.

Let's delve into these factors and uncover why savoring life's experiences can lead to greater satisfaction than the endless pursuit of material possessions.

Psychological Impact: The Joy of Doing vs. Having

Meet Alex, a 28-year-old software developer. For years, Alex saved diligently to buy a luxury sports car, believing it would bring him happiness. When he finally made the purchase, he felt an initial surge of excitement. However, this joy quickly faded as the car became just another part of his daily routine.

Contrast this with Alex's decision to use his next bonus for a two-week hiking trip in the Andes. The anticipation leading up to the trip, the awe-inspiring moments during the journey, and the memories he cherished long after returning home provided a more profound and lasting sense of fulfillment.

Alex's story illustrates a key psychological principle: experiences tend to provide more enduring happiness than material possessions. This is partly because we adapt quickly to new possessions, a phenomenon known as hedonic adaptation. Experiences, on the other hand, become a part of our identity and provide lasting memories.

Long-term Value: The Gift That Keeps on Giving

Consider the case of Emma, a 40-year-old marketing executive. Emma used to spend much of her disposable income on designer clothes and accessories. While each purchase brought a momentary thrill, she often found herself wanting more, trapped in a cycle of constant acquisition.

A turning point came when Emma decided to invest in experiences instead. She took cooking classes, traveled to new countries, and attended concerts of her favorite artists. These experiences not only provided immediate joy but also equipped her with new skills, broadened her perspectives, and created stories she could share for years to come.

Emma's shift in focus demonstrates the long-term value of experiences. Unlike material possessions that depreciate or become obsolete, the value of experiences often appreciates over time. Our memories tend to become fonder, and the skills and perspectives gained from experiences continue to enrich our lives long after the event has passed.

The Social Dimension of Experiences

An often overlooked aspect of experiences is their social nature. Let's look at the story of the Johnson family. Instead of buying each other expensive gifts for Christmas, they decided to take a family trip to a national park. The shared adventure not only created enduring memories but also deepened their family bonds.

This example highlights how experiences often involve other people, fostering social connections and shared memories. These social bonds contribute significantly to our overall life satisfaction, further enhancing the value of experiences over solo material acquisitions.

Balancing Experiences and Possessions

While the focus of this subchapter is on the value of experiences, it's important to note that some material possessions can enhance our ability to have meaningful experiences. For instance, a good pair of hiking boots can enable more enjoyable outdoor adventures.

The key is to be mindful of the purpose behind our purchases. Are we buying something solely for the sake of ownership, or will it facilitate valuable experiences and personal growth?

Actionable Tips and Exercises:

1. Experience Wish List: Create a list of experiences you'd like to have in the next year. These could range from learning a new skill to visiting a new place. Prioritize this list and start planning for the top items.

2. Possession Purpose Audit: Go through your recent purchases and evaluate each item. Consider asking yourself, "Has this improved my experiences or quality of life?" Use this insight to guide future purchasing decisions.

3. Memory Savoring Practice: Each day for a week, spend 5 minutes recalling a positive experience from your past. Notice how this affects your mood compared to thinking about material possessions.

4. Experience Investment Plan: Allocate a portion of your discretionary income specifically for experiences. Start with 10% and adjust based on what feels right for your situation.

5. Shared Experience Challenge: Plan an experience to share with loved ones, focusing on quality time and creating memories rather than spending money. Reflect on how this impacts your relationships and overall satisfaction.

By engaging with these exercises, you can start to shift your focus towards experiences that provide lasting fulfillment and enrich your life in meaningful ways.

To sum up, while material possessions have their place, savoring life's experiences often proves more rewarding in the long run. By understanding the psychological impact and long-term value of experiences, we can make more informed choices about how we invest our time and resources, ultimately leading to a richer, more satisfying life.

Chapter 8: Having an Intentional Relationship With Money

Money: it's a tool, a resource, and for many, a source of both opportunity and anxiety. But what if we could transform our relationship with money from one of passive reaction to active intention? This chapter explores the powerful concept of developing an intentional relationship with your finances.

At its core, an intentional relationship with money revolves around two key factors:

1. Conscious Decision-Making: Making deliberate choices about earning, spending, saving, and investing.
2. Alignment with Personal Values: Ensuring that financial decisions reflect and support your core beliefs and life goals.

Throughout this chapter, we'll delve into how these factors interplay to create a more meaningful and purposeful approach to managing your finances.

Consider for a moment: How often do you make financial decisions on autopilot? From daily coffee purchases to major investments, our financial lives are often guided by habit rather than conscious choice. By shifting to an intentional approach, we can harness the power of money to support our deepest aspirations and values.

This intentional relationship isn't about penny-pinching or obsessive budgeting. Instead, it's about creating a thoughtful framework that allows money to serve you, rather than the other way around. It's about understanding that every financial decision is, at its heart, a life decision. As we progress through this chapter, we'll explore practical strategies for cultivating this intentional relationship. We'll examine how to identify your core values and align them with your financial choices. We'll also dive into techniques for making more conscious decisions about money, from everyday purchases to long-term financial planning.

You'll discover how an intentional approach can reduce financial stress, increase satisfaction with your spending, and help you achieve your most important life goals. Whether you're just starting your financial journey or looking to refine your approach, this chapter offers valuable insights for everyone.

Get ready to transform your relationship with money. By the end of this chapter, you'll have the tools to approach your finances with greater clarity, purpose, and intention. This shift promises not just to change how you manage your money, but how you view its role in creating the life you truly desire.

8.1: Right-Sizing Your Money Mindset

Developing an intentional relationship with money begins with understanding and adjusting your money mindset. This subchapter explores how to "right-size" your approach to finances, creating a balanced perspective that aligns with your values and goals. We'll focus on two main factors:

1. **Self-Awareness:** Recognizing your current beliefs and attitudes about money.
2. **Mindset Flexibility:** Developing the ability to adapt your financial thinking as circumstances change.

Let's dive into these factors and examine how they contribute to a healthier, more intentional relationship with money.

Self-Awareness: Uncovering Your Money Beliefs

Meet Lisa, a 32-year-old graphic designer. Despite earning a comfortable income, Lisa always felt anxious about money. She'd grown up in a household where money was tight, and her parents often argued about finances. As a result, Lisa developed a scarcity mindset, always fearing that she didn't have enough, even when her bank account suggested otherwise.

Through self-reflection and therapy, Lisa realized how her childhood experiences shaped her current money attitudes. This awareness was the first step in changing her relationship with money. She began to challenge her ingrained beliefs and gradually developed a more balanced perspective.

Lisa's story highlights the importance of self-awareness in shaping our money mindset. Our past experiences, family attitudes, and cultural influences all play a role in forming our financial beliefs. By recognizing these influences, we can begin to question whether they serve us well in our current circumstances.

Mindset Flexibility: Adapting to Change

Now, consider the case of Mark, a 45-year-old former corporate executive. Mark had always equated money with success and security. His high-paying job allowed him to live a luxurious lifestyle, which he saw as a testament to his worth.

However, when Mark lost his job during a company restructuring, his rigid money mindset became a liability. He struggled to adapt to his new financial reality, clinging to his previous lifestyle and quickly depleting his savings. It wasn't until Mark embraced a more flexible mindset that he was able to adjust his spending, explore new career opportunities, and ultimately find fulfillment in a less lucrative but more personally rewarding field.

Mark's experience demonstrates the importance of mindset flexibility. Life circumstances change, and our approach to money needs to evolve accordingly. A flexible money mindset allows us to adapt to new situations without losing sight of our core values and long-term goals.

The Interplay of Self-Awareness and Flexibility

These two factors - self-awareness and mindset flexibility - work together to create a robust, adaptable money mindset. Let's look at the example of Sarah, a 38-year-old entrepreneur, to see how this interplay works in practice.

Sarah grew up in a family that valued financial security above all else. This led her to initially choose a stable but unfulfilling corporate career. Through self-reflection, Sarah recognized this influence on her choices. With this awareness, she was able to challenge her ingrained beliefs and develop the flexibility to consider other options.

Sarah eventually left her corporate job to start her own business. While this move involved financial uncertainty, her newfound mindset flexibility allowed her to see money as a tool for creating the life she wanted, rather than just a measure of security. Her self-awareness helped her navigate the emotional challenges of this transition, while her flexible mindset enabled her to adapt her financial strategies as her business grew.

Balancing Prudence and Possibility

Right-sizing your money mindset isn't about swinging from one extreme to another. It's about finding a balance between prudent financial management and openness to possibilities. This balance allows you to make sound financial decisions while remaining open to opportunities that align with your values and goals.

Actionable Tips and Exercises:

1. Money Memory Journal: Write about your earliest money memories. Reflect on how these experiences might be influencing your current attitudes towards money.

2. Belief Audit: List your top five beliefs about money. For each belief, reflect: 'Is this serving me effectively?" Where did this belief come from? Is it based on current reality or past experiences?"

3. Mindset Flexibility Challenge: Identify a recent financial decision or situation where you felt stuck. Brainstorm three alternative perspectives or approaches you could have taken.

4. Values-Money Alignment Check: List your top five personal values. Then, review your recent financial decisions. How well do they align with these values? Identify one area where you could better align your spending with your values.

5. Financial "What If" Scenarios: Create three hypothetical financial scenarios (e.g., a 50% income increase, a 30% income decrease, a major unexpected expense). For each, outline how you would adapt your financial approach. This exercise helps develop mindset flexibility.

By engaging with these exercises, you can begin to cultivate greater self-awareness and flexibility in your money mindset. Remember, right-sizing your money mindset is an ongoing process. It requires regular reflection and adjustment as your life circumstances and financial goals evolve.

To wrap up, developing the right money mindset is crucial for creating an intentional relationship with your finances. By fostering self-awareness and cultivating mindset flexibility, you can create a balanced approach to money that supports your values, adapts to changing circumstances, and ultimately helps you achieve your most important life goals.

8.2: Lifestyle Practices for Genuine Wealth

Having explored the importance of right-sizing your money mindset, let's now turn our attention to practical lifestyle choices that can foster genuine wealth. In this subchapter, we'll examine how daily habits and long-term practices can contribute to a sense of abundance that goes beyond mere financial metrics. We'll focus on two main factors:

1. Mindful Consumption: Making intentional choices about how we spend our resources.
2. Value-Driven Investments: Allocating our time and money in ways that align with our core values.

Let's delve into these factors and see how they can shape a lifestyle of genuine wealth.

Mindful Consumption: Quality Over Quantity

Meet Jamie, a 29-year-old marketing professional. Jamie used to be caught in a cycle of impulse buying, constantly chasing the latest trends and gadgets. Her apartment was cluttered with barely-used items, and her credit card debt was mounting. Despite her frequent purchases, Jamie felt a persistent sense of lack.

A turning point came when Jamie stumbled upon the concept of minimalism. She began to question each purchase, asking herself, "Will this truly add value to my life?" Over time, Jamie decluttered her space and became more selective in her consumption. To her surprise, she found that owning fewer, higher-quality items not only saved her money but also increased her overall satisfaction.

Jamie's story illustrates the power of mindful consumption. By shifting focus from quantity to quality, we can reduce unnecessary spending, decrease clutter, and increase our appreciation for what we have. This approach often leads to a greater sense of contentment and financial well-being.

Value-Driven Investments: Time and Money Well Spent

Now, let's consider the case of Robert, a 42-year-old software engineer. Robert earned a substantial income but felt unfulfilled. He spent long hours at work, leaving little time for his family or personal interests. His expensive car and luxurious apartment, meant to be symbols of success, felt hollow.

Inspired by a colleague's sabbatical experience, Robert decided to reassess his priorities. He realized that his core values centered around family, personal growth, and community service. With this clarity, Robert made some bold changes. He negotiated a four-day work week, accepting a pay cut in exchange for more family time. He also started volunteering at a local coding bootcamp and invested in experiences that brought his family closer together.

Robert's shift to value-driven investments dramatically improved his sense of wealth and fulfillment. While his bank balance may have decreased slightly, his overall quality of life improved significantly.

The Interplay of Mindful Consumption and Value-Driven Investments

These two factors - mindful consumption and value-driven investments - work in tandem to create a lifestyle of genuine wealth. Let's look at the example of Maria, a 35-year-old teacher, to see how this interplay manifests in real life.

Maria adopted a mindful consumption approach, carefully considering each purchase and focusing on quality over quantity. This practice freed up resources - both money and mental energy - which she then reinvested in areas aligned with her values. She used her savings to enroll in a master's program she'd always dreamed of pursuing, and allocated more time to nurturing her relationships.

The result was a virtuous cycle: mindful consumption created space for value-driven investments, which in turn reinforced the benefits of mindful consumption. Maria found herself feeling wealthier and more fulfilled, despite not seeing a significant change in her income.

Redefining Wealth: Beyond the Balance Sheet

Adopting these lifestyle practices requires us to expand our definition of wealth beyond mere financial metrics. True wealth encompasses not just monetary assets, but also rich experiences, strong relationships, personal growth, and a sense of purpose.

By practicing mindful consumption and making value-driven investments, we can cultivate a sense of abundance that isn't dependent on continual acquisition or a specific income level. This approach allows us to experience genuine wealth, regardless of our financial circumstances.

Actionable Tips and Exercises:

1. **Consumption Journal:** For one week, record every purchase you make. For each item, note whether it was a need or a want, and rate how much value it added to your life on a scale of 1-10. Use this data to identify areas where you can practice more mindful consumption.

2. **Value-Money Alignment Audit:** List your top five personal values. Then, review your bank statements from the last three months.

What percentage of your spending aligns with each value? Identify one area where you could better align your spending with your values.

3. Time Budget Exercise: Track how you spend your time for a week. Then, create an ideal "time budget" that reflects your values and priorities. Identify one change you can make this week to bring your actual time use closer to your ideal.

4. Quality Assessment: Choose three items you use regularly. Research high-quality, durable alternatives that might be more expensive upfront but could save money in the long run. Consider whether these upgrades would align with your mindful consumption goals.

5. Experience Investment Plan: Allocate a portion of your discretionary income specifically for experiences that align with your values (e.g., learning a new skill, family activities, travel). Start with 5% and adjust based on what feels right for your situation.

By engaging with these exercises, you can begin to implement lifestyle practices that foster genuine wealth. Remember, this is a gradual process. Small, consistent changes can lead to significant shifts in your experience of wealth and fulfillment over time.

To sum up, cultivating genuine wealth goes beyond accumulating money. By practicing mindful consumption and making value-driven investments of our time and resources, we can create a lifestyle that feels truly rich and fulfilling. These practices allow us to experience abundance in all areas of life, leading to a more holistic and satisfying definition of wealth.

Chapter 9: Money's Potential Upside

Money often gets a bad rap. It's blamed for greed, inequality, and a host of societal ills. But what if we looked at money through a different lens? What if we explored its potential as a force for good? This chapter invites you to reconsider money's role in creating positive change, both in your personal life and in the world at large.

At its core, money's potential upside revolves around two key factors:

1. Empowerment: How money can enable personal growth and self-actualization.
2. Impact: The capacity of financial resources to drive positive societal change.

Throughout this chapter, we'll delve into these factors, uncovering how they can transform our relationship with money and amplify its positive potential.

Think about it: When used wisely, money can fund education, support dreams, provide security, and even save lives. It can be the seed that grows into a world-changing innovation or the lifeline that sustains vital community services.

But this isn't about viewing money through rose-tinted glasses. It's about recognizing its power as a tool and learning how to wield that tool effectively and ethically. By understanding money's potential upside, we can make more intentional choices about earning, spending, saving, and giving.

As we progress through this chapter, we'll explore real-world examples of individuals and organizations harnessing money's positive potential. We'll examine strategies for aligning your financial decisions with your values and goals. And we'll discuss how to maximize the impact of your resources, whether abundant or modest.

You'll discover that money's potential upside isn't reserved for the wealthy. Everyone, regardless of their financial situation, has the power to use money as a force for good. Whether it's through mindful spending, strategic saving, or purposeful giving, each of us can tap into money's potential to create positive change.

Get ready to see money in a new light. By the end of this chapter, you'll have a fresh perspective on the role of money in your life and society. This shift in viewpoint promises not just to change how you manage your finances, but how you perceive money's capacity to shape a better future for yourself and others.

9.1: When Money Increases Well-Being

While money itself doesn't guarantee happiness, it can significantly enhance our well-being when used thoughtfully. This subchapter explores the ways in which financial resources can positively impact our lives and the lives of others. We'll focus on two main factors:

1. **Basic Needs Fulfillment:** How money can secure fundamental necessities and reduce stress.
2. **Experiential Investments:** The role of money in funding meaningful experiences and personal growth.

Let's delve into these factors and examine how they contribute to increased well-being.

Basic Needs Fulfillment: The Foundation of Well-Being

Meet Sarah, a 28-year-old freelance writer. For years, Sarah struggled to make ends meet, constantly worrying about paying rent and buying groceries. This financial stress took a toll on her mental health and creativity. When Sarah landed a lucrative contract, she was finally able to cover her basic needs comfortably. The relief was palpable. With her fundamental needs met, Sarah's anxiety decreased, her sleep improved, and her creative output flourished.

Sarah's story illustrates how money can significantly increase well-being by fulfilling basic needs. When we're not constantly worried about survival, we have the mental and emotional bandwidth to focus on other aspects of life. This security forms the foundation upon which we can build a fulfilling life.

Research supports this concept. A famous study by Nobel laureates Daniel Kahneman and Angus Deaton found that emotional well-being rises with income, up to a certain point. This point, often referred to as the "satiation point," varies by location and individual circumstances, but it underscores the importance of having enough to cover basic needs and a bit more for comfort.

Experiential Investments: Beyond the Basics

Now, let's consider the case of Marco, a 35-year-old software engineer. Marco had a comfortable income that easily covered his basic needs. However, he felt unfulfilled, spending most of his disposable income on material possessions that provided only fleeting satisfaction. Inspired by a friend's transformative travel experience, Marco decided to invest in experiences instead.

He used his savings to take a sabbatical, during which he volunteered in various countries, learned new languages, and immersed himself in different cultures. These experiences broadened his perspective, developed new skills, and created lasting memories. Marco returned to work rejuvenated, with a newfound sense of purpose and connection to the world.

Marco's story highlights how money can increase well-being through experiential investments. Research has consistently shown that spending money on experiences tends to provide more lasting happiness than material purchases. Experiences contribute to personal growth, create stories we can share, and often involve social connections - all factors that significantly contribute to well-being.

The Interplay of Basic Needs and Experiential Investments

These two factors - basic needs fulfillment and experiential investments - work together to maximize the positive impact of money on well-being. Let's look at the example of Elena, a 40-year-old teacher, to see how this interplay works in practice.

Elena inherited a modest sum from her grandmother. Instead of splurging on luxury items, she made strategic choices. First, she paid off her debts, which had been a source of constant stress. This addressed her basic need for financial security. With the remaining money, Elena enrolled in a summer course in Italy to enhance her teaching skills and indulge her passion for art history.

By addressing both her basic needs and investing in a meaningful experience, Elena maximized the well-being boost from her inheritance. The debt repayment provided long-term peace of mind, while the course offered personal growth, new connections, and cherished memories.

Balancing Present and Future Well-Being

When using money to increase well-being, it's crucial to balance present enjoyment with future security. This balance allows us to experience the benefits of our resources now, while also ensuring continued well-being in the future.

For instance, setting aside money for retirement or an emergency fund might not provide immediate pleasure, but it significantly contributes to overall well-being by reducing future stress and uncertainty. Similarly, investing in health - through nutritious food, exercise, or preventive care - may require financial resources now but pays dividends in long-term well-being.

Actionable Tips and Exercises:

1. Basic Needs Audit: List your basic needs (e.g., housing, food, healthcare). Rate how well each is currently met on a scale of 1-10. Recognize areas for improvement and develop a plan to address them.

2. Experiential Wishlist: Create a list of experiences you believe would enhance your well-being (e.g., learning a new skill, traveling to a specific location). Prioritize this list and start planning for the top item.

3. Happiness Per Dollar Exercise: For your last five significant purchases, divide the happiness or satisfaction they've provided (rate from 1-10) by the amount spent. This will provide you with a "happiness-to-dollar" ratio. Use this to inform future spending decisions.

4. Future Well-Being Investment: Identify one area where investing money now could significantly improve your future well-being (e.g., education, health, retirement savings). Create a specific, actionable plan to start this investment.

5. Gratitude Practice: Each day for a week, write down three ways money has positively impacted your well-being. This exercise can help shift your perspective and increase appreciation for the resources you have.

By engaging with these exercises, you can begin to more intentionally use money to increase your well-being. Remember, the goal is not to maximize spending, but to optimize the impact of your financial resources on your overall quality of life.

To wrap up, money can indeed increase well-being when used thoughtfully. By ensuring our basic needs are met and investing in meaningful experiences, we can harness the positive potential of our financial resources. The key is to make conscious choices that align with our values and contribute to both our present happiness and future security.

9.2: Using Wealth for Good

Having explored how money can enhance personal well-being, let's now turn our attention to its potential for creating positive change on a broader scale. This subchapter delves into the ways we can leverage our financial resources, regardless of their magnitude, to benefit society and the world at large. We'll focus on two main factors:

1. Strategic Giving: How thoughtful philanthropy can maximize impact.
2. Conscious Consumption: The power of aligning spending with values.

Let's examine these factors and see how they can transform wealth into a force for good.

Strategic Giving: Maximizing Philanthropic Impact

Meet Lisa, a 45-year-old small business owner. Lisa had always donated to various charities, but she often felt her contributions were just drops in a vast ocean of need. Determined to make a more significant impact, Lisa decided to approach her giving strategically.

She researched extensively, focusing on causes close to her heart. Lisa discovered a local education initiative that provided coding classes to underprivileged youth. Instead of spreading her donations thinly across multiple charities, she concentrated her resources on this program. Lisa's targeted approach allowed her to fund an entire year of classes for 20 students.

By volunteering her time as well, Lisa saw firsthand the transformative effect of her strategic giving. Several students went on to pursue careers in technology, breaking the cycle of poverty in their families.

Lisa's story illustrates the power of strategic giving. By focusing our resources and combining financial support with personal involvement, we can amplify the impact of our philanthropy. This approach allows us to see tangible results and feel more connected to the causes we support.

Conscious Consumption: Voting with Our Dollars

Now, let's consider the case of Alex, a 32-year-old marketing executive. Alex had always been passionate about environmental conservation but felt his individual actions were insignificant in the face of global challenges. Then, Alex learned about the concept of conscious consumption.

He began researching the companies he bought from, prioritizing those with strong environmental and ethical practices. Alex switched to a renewable energy provider, started buying from B Corps, and invested in a sustainable fashion brand. He also opened an account with a credit union that invested in local green initiatives.

While these changes seemed small at first, Alex soon realized the cumulative impact. His choices supported businesses aligned with his values, encouraging more companies to adopt sustainable practices.

Moreover, Alex's example inspired friends and colleagues to make similar shifts in their consumption habits.

Alex's story demonstrates how conscious consumption can turn everyday transactions into opportunities for positive change. By aligning our spending with our values, we can support businesses and practices that contribute to the greater good.

The Synergy of Strategic Giving and Conscious Consumption

These two factors - strategic giving and conscious consumption - work in tandem to maximize the positive impact of our wealth. Let's look at the example of Maria and John, a couple in their 50s, to see how this synergy operates in practice.

Maria and John had always been careful with their money, building a comfortable nest egg over the years. As they approached retirement, they decided to use their wealth more purposefully. They adopted a two-pronged approach:

First, they identified a local food security program as their primary philanthropic focus. They made substantial donations and volunteered regularly, helping the program expand its reach to more families in need.

Second, they overhauled their spending habits. They switched to a bank that supported small businesses, started shopping at farmer's markets to support local agriculture, and invested in companies with strong social responsibility records.

By combining strategic giving with conscious consumption, Maria and John created a holistic approach to using their wealth for good. Their targeted philanthropy made a significant impact on food security in their community, while their everyday spending choices supported a more sustainable and equitable economy.

Wealth as a Tool for Change: Beyond the Numbers

It's crucial to remember that using wealth for good isn't solely about the amount of money we have. Even modest financial resources, when used thoughtfully, can create ripples of positive change.

Consider the story of Aisha, a college student working part-time. Despite her limited income, Aisha was passionate about animal welfare. She couldn't make large donations, but she found other ways to contribute. Aisha used a round-up app that donated her spare change to animal shelters. She also chose a credit card that gave cash back to wildlife conservation efforts.

These small, consistent actions allowed Aisha to support causes she cared about without straining her budget. Over time, her contributions added up, demonstrating that everyone, regardless of their wealth level, can use their financial resources for good.

Actionable Tips and Exercises:

1. Cause Identification Exercise: List three issues you're passionate about. Research organizations working in these areas. Identify one where you believe your support (financial or otherwise) could make a tangible difference.

2. Giving Plan: Create a giving budget. Decide what percentage of your income you can comfortably donate. Consider setting up automatic monthly donations to your chosen cause.

3. Conscious Consumption Audit: Review your regular purchases (groceries, utilities, clothes, etc.). Identify three areas where you could switch to more ethical or sustainable options. Research alternatives and make a plan to transition.

4. Impact Investment Research: Look into impact investment options available to you (e.g., socially responsible mutual funds, community investment notes). Select one to start with, even if it's a small amount.

5. Skill-Based Volunteering: List your professional skills or hobbies. Research organizations in your area that could benefit from these skills. Commit to offering your expertise for a specific project or time period.

By engaging with these exercises, you can start to more intentionally use your wealth - whatever its size - as a force for good. Remember, the goal is not to deplete your resources, but to align your financial decisions with your values and desire to make a positive impact.

To round off, using wealth for good is about more than just donating to charity. It involves a holistic approach that encompasses strategic giving, conscious consumption, and recognizing the power of even small financial decisions. By thoughtfully leveraging our resources, we can create meaningful change and contribute to a better world, all while deriving a deeper sense of purpose and fulfillment from our wealth.

Chapter 10: Psychological Theories of Money and Happiness

Money and happiness - two concepts that have captivated philosophers, economists, and psychologists for centuries. Are they inextricably linked, or do they dance to different tunes? In this chapter, we'll dive deep into the fascinating world of psychological theories that attempt to unravel the complex relationship between wealth and well-being.

At the heart of our exploration lie two key factors:

1. Cognitive Perspectives: How our thoughts and beliefs about money shape our happiness.

2. Emotional Responses: The way our feelings interact with financial situations and outcomes.

These factors form the foundation of our understanding, guiding us through a maze of research, theories, and real-world applications.

As we embark on this journey, prepare to challenge your preconceptions. You might find that some commonly held beliefs about money and happiness don't quite stand up to scientific scrutiny. Conversely, you may discover surprising connections that shed new light on your own experiences with wealth and contentment.

We'll examine groundbreaking studies that have shaped our understanding of financial psychology. From the hedonic treadmill theory to the concept of relative income, each idea offers a unique lens through which to view the money-happiness equation.

But this isn't just an academic exercise. Throughout the chapter, we'll explore how these theories play out in everyday life. You'll see how understanding these concepts can empower you to make more informed decisions about your finances and potentially boost your overall life satisfaction.

Get ready to delve into questions like: Does more money always lead to greater happiness? How do our financial goals influence our well-being? What role does comparison play in our financial satisfaction? And perhaps most importantly, how can we apply these insights to lead more fulfilling lives?

By the time you reach the end of this chapter, you'll have a richer understanding of the psychological underpinnings of money and happiness. This knowledge isn't just intellectually stimulating - it's a powerful tool for personal growth and financial well-being.

So, let's set off on this enlightening exploration. The intersection of money and happiness awaits, filled with insights that could transform your perspective on wealth, contentment, and the good life.

10.1: Maslow's Hierarchy of Needs and Financial Well-Being

Abraham Maslow's Hierarchy of Needs is a cornerstone of psychological theory that offers valuable insights into the relationship between money and happiness. This subchapter explores how financial well-being intersects with Maslow's framework, focusing on two main factors:

1. **Need Fulfillment:** How money facilitates the satisfaction of various levels of needs.
2. **Psychological Progression:** The role of financial security in moving up the hierarchy.

Let's delve into these factors and examine how they influence our financial well-being and overall happiness.

Need Fulfillment: Money as a Tool for Satisfaction

Maslow's hierarchy consists of five levels: physiological needs, safety needs, love and belonging, esteem, and self-actualization. Money plays a crucial role in satisfying these needs, particularly at the lower levels.

Consider the story of Tom, a recent college graduate struggling to make ends meet. Tom's entry-level salary barely covered his rent and groceries, leaving him constantly stressed about basic survival. In Maslow's terms, Tom was stuck at the physiological needs level, unable to focus on higher pursuits.

When Tom received a promotion and pay raise, he experienced a significant shift. He could now afford a safer apartment in a better neighborhood and build an emergency fund. This financial boost allowed Tom to progress to the safety needs level, reducing his stress and opening up mental space for personal growth.

Tom's experience illustrates how money can be a powerful tool for satisfying lower-level needs. As we move up the hierarchy, the role of money becomes more nuanced but remains significant.

Psychological Progression: Financial Security as a Stepping Stone

Let's now turn to the case of Sarah, a mid-career professional with a stable income. Sarah's financial situation allowed her to comfortably meet her physiological and safety needs. This security enabled her to focus on love and belonging, investing time and resources into building meaningful relationships and community involvement.

As Sarah's career advanced, she gained recognition for her expertise, satisfying her esteem needs. With a robust financial foundation, Sarah felt confident enough to pursue her passion for painting, moving towards self-actualization.

Sarah's journey demonstrates how financial well-being can facilitate progression through Maslow's hierarchy. By providing a sense of security, money allows individuals to direct their energy towards higher-level needs and personal fulfillment.

The Interplay of Need Fulfillment and Psychological Progression

These two factors - require fulfillment and psychological progression - work in tandem to shape our financial well-being and overall happiness. Let's examine the case of the Johnson family to see this interplay in action.

The Johnsons, a middle-class family of four, had always prioritized financial stability. They lived below their means, built an emergency fund, and invested in their children's education. This approach ensured their physiological and safety needs were consistently met.

With this solid foundation, the Johnsons could focus on strengthening family bonds and community connections, addressing their love and belonging needs. They invested time and resources in family vacations and local community projects.

As their children grew and their careers advanced, the Johnsons found themselves in a position to pursue personal interests and give back to their community, moving towards esteem and self-actualization.

The Johnson family's story highlights how financial decisions aligned with Maslow's hierarchy can lead to a more balanced and fulfilling life. By strategically using their resources to address needs at each level, they created a pathway for continuous personal and collective growth.

Beyond Basic Needs: Money and Higher-Level Satisfaction

While money is crucial for satisfying lower-level needs, its relationship with higher-level needs is more complex. Once basic needs are met, the impact of additional income on happiness tends to diminish - a phenomenon known as the "hedonic treadmill."

However, money can still play a significant role in achieving higher-level satisfaction when used intentionally. For instance, it can fund educational pursuits, enable career changes aligned with personal values, or support philanthropic efforts - all of which contribute to esteem and self-actualization.

Consider Elena, a successful executive who felt unfulfilled despite her high salary. Elena decided to use her financial security as a launchpad for change. She reduced her work hours, accepting a pay cut, to pursue a degree in environmental science - her true passion. While her income decreased, her sense of purpose and fulfillment grew tremendously.

Elena's story demonstrates that aligning financial decisions with higher-level needs can lead to greater happiness and life satisfaction, even if it doesn't always mean earning more money.

Actionable Tips and Exercises:

1. Needs Assessment: List your current needs according to Maslow's hierarchy. Rate how well each need is being met on a scale of 1-10. Identify areas where financial resources could help improve satisfaction.

2. Financial Goal Alignment: Review your financial goals. How do they align with different levels of Maslow's hierarchy? Adjust your goals to ensure you're addressing needs at all levels.

3. Resource Allocation Exercise: Divide your monthly income into categories corresponding to Maslow's hierarchy levels. Are you overinvesting in one area while neglecting others? Brainstorm ways to create a more balanced allocation.

4. Higher-Level Need Exploration: Identify one higher-level need (esteem or self-actualization) you'd like to pursue. Create a financial plan to support this goal, even if it's a small step like setting aside funds for a class or workshop.

5. Gratitude and Reflection Practice: Each day for a week, write down one way your current financial situation has allowed you to meet a need or pursue a higher-level goal. This can help shift focus from what you lack to what you've achieved.

By engaging with these exercises, you can start to more consciously align your financial decisions with Maslow's hierarchy, potentially enhancing both your financial well-being and overall life satisfaction.

To sum up, Maslow's Hierarchy of Needs provides a valuable framework for understanding the relationship between money and well-being. By recognizing how financial resources can support need fulfillment and psychological progression, we can make more intentional choices about earning, spending, and saving. The key is to use money as a tool for holistic growth, addressing needs at all levels of the hierarchy in pursuit of a balanced, fulfilling life.

10.2: Self-Determination Theory: How Money Affects Autonomy, Competence, and Relatedness

Self-Determination Theory (SDT), developed by psychologists Edward Deci and Richard Ryan, provides a compelling framework for understanding how money influences our psychological well-being. This subchapter explores the intricate relationship between financial resources and the three core needs identified by SDT: autonomy, competence, and relatedness. We'll focus on two main factors:

1. Financial Empowerment: How money can enhance or hinder our sense of autonomy and competence.

2. Monetary Influence on Relationships: The impact of financial status on our connections with others.

Let's delve into these factors and examine how they shape our motivations, behaviors, and overall satisfaction in life.

Financial Empowerment: Money's Role in Autonomy and Competence

Autonomy, in SDT, refers to our need to feel in control of our own lives and actions. Competence relates to our desire to master skills and feel effective in our endeavors. Money can significantly influence both of these needs.

Take into account the story of Alex, a young graphic designer. Fresh out of college, Alex took a job at a large advertising firm. The salary was impressive, but the work was creatively stifling. Despite financial security, Alex felt a lack of autonomy in decision-making and couldn't fully utilize his skills.

After two years, Alex decided to take a risk. He quit his job to start a freelance design business. Initially, his income dropped dramatically, causing stress. However, as he built his client base, Alex experienced a profound shift. He had the freedom to choose projects that aligned with his values and could fully apply his creativity. His sense of autonomy soared, and as he honed his skills, his feeling of competence grew as well.

Alex's journey illustrates how money can both support and hinder autonomy and competence. While his high-paying job provided financial security, it limited his autonomy. The initial financial struggle of freelancing was challenging, but ultimately led to greater satisfaction of his core psychological needs.

Monetary Influence on Relationships: The Relatedness Factor

Relatedness, the third pillar of SDT, concerns our need for meaningful connections with others. Money's impact on this aspect of well-being is complex and often overlooked.

Let's examine the case of the Martinez family. Carlos and Maria Martinez were hardworking immigrants who prioritized financial stability to provide opportunities for their children. Their dedication paid off, and they achieved significant financial success. However, this pursuit came at a cost – long work hours meant less time for family bonding and community involvement.

As their financial situation improved, the Martinezes realized the importance of balancing wealth accumulation with relationship nurturing. They made a conscious decision to adjust their work-life balance, using their financial resources to create meaningful family experiences and engage more with their community.

This shift allowed them to satisfy their need for relatedness without sacrificing the financial security they had worked hard to achieve. They found that money, when used wisely, could enhance their relationships rather than detract from them.

The Interplay of Financial Empowerment and Relational Influence

These two factors – financial empowerment and monetary influence on relationships – often interact in nuanced ways. Let's look at the story of Sarah, a mid-career professional, to see this interplay in action.

Sarah had always been career-focused, climbing the corporate ladder with determination. Her rising income allowed her to feel increasingly competent and autonomous in her personal life. She could afford to pursue hobbies, travel, and make independent life choices.

However, Sarah began to notice a sense of disconnection. Her busy schedule and financial disparity with old friends strained some relationships. Recognizing this, Sarah used her financial resources and newfound autonomy to rekindle and deepen connections. She organized reunions, supported friends in need, and engaged in philanthropic activities that aligned with her values.

Through this process, Sarah found a balance between using money to support her autonomy and competence while also nurturing her need for relatedness. Her story demonstrates how financial resources, when mindfully managed, can positively impact all three core needs identified by Self-Determination Theory.

Beyond the Numbers: Intrinsic vs. Extrinsic Goals

An essential aspect of SDT is the distinction between intrinsic and extrinsic goals. Intrinsic goals, such as personal growth and community contribution, tend to satisfy our core needs more effectively than extrinsic goals like wealth accumulation or status.

Consider Tom, a successful entrepreneur. Initially driven by the extrinsic goal of becoming wealthy, Tom achieved financial success but felt unfulfilled. After learning about SDT, he shifted his focus to more intrinsic goals. He used his wealth to fund educational programs in underserved communities, satisfying his needs for competence and relatedness. He also allocated time and resources to personal development, enhancing his sense of autonomy.

Tom's reorientation towards intrinsic goals led to a more profound sense of well-being, illustrating how the application of money in alignment with SDT principles can lead to greater life satisfaction.

Actionable Tips and Exercises:
  1. Autonomy Audit: List three areas in your life where you feel a lack of control. Brainstorm how you could use your financial resources (even if limited) to increase your autonomy in these areas.

  2. Competence Development Plan: Identify a skill you'd like to improve. Create a budget for resources (classes, books, tools) that could help you develop this competence.

  3. Relationship Investment Strategy: Allocate a portion of your monthly budget specifically for nurturing relationships. This could include funds for social activities, gifts, or supporting causes that matter to your loved ones.

  4. Intrinsic vs. Extrinsic Goal Assessment: Write down your top five financial goals. Categorize them as intrinsic or extrinsic. For any extrinsic goals, try to reframe them in terms of intrinsic motivations.

  5. Weekly Well-being Check: At the end of each week, rate your sense of autonomy, competence, and relatedness on a scale of 1-10. Reflect on how your financial decisions that week impacted these ratings.

By engaging with these exercises, you can start to align your financial decisions more closely with the principles of Self-Determination Theory, potentially enhancing your overall well-being and life satisfaction.

To wrap up, Self-Determination Theory offers a valuable lens through which to view the relationship between money and psychological well-being. By understanding how financial resources can impact our sense of autonomy, competence, and relatedness, we can make more intentional choices about how we earn, spend, and save. The key is to use money as a tool to support intrinsic goals and satisfy core psychological needs, rather than viewing wealth accumulation as an end in itself. With this approach, we can harness the power of our financial resources to lead more fulfilling and psychologically balanced lives.

10.3: Prospect Theory: Risk, Loss Aversion, and Financial Decision-Making

Prospect Theory, developed by psychologists Daniel Kahneman and Amos Tversky, revolutionized our understanding of how people make decisions under uncertainty. This subchapter explores how Prospect Theory illuminates our financial choices, focusing on two main factors:

1. Loss Aversion: Our tendency to feel the pain of losses more acutely than the pleasure of equivalent gains.
2. Reference Points: How our perception of outcomes as gains or losses depends on our starting point.

Let's delve into these factors and examine how they shape our financial behaviors and decision-making processes.

Loss Aversion: The Asymmetry of Financial Pain and Pleasure
Loss aversion is a cornerstone of Prospect Theory, suggesting that the negative impact of losing a sum of money is psychologically more powerful than the positive impact of gaining the same amount.

Consider the story of Emily, a small business owner. When faced with the choice between a guaranteed $5,000 grant or a 50% chance of winning a $10,000 grant, Emily opted for the sure thing. However, when later confronted with a certain $5,000 loss or a 50% chance of losing $10,000, she chose the risky option.

Emily's decisions perfectly illustrate loss aversion. In the realm of gains, she played it safe, but when facing losses, she was willing to take risks to avoid the certain loss. This asymmetry in risk attitudes between gains and losses is a hallmark of human decision-making, often leading to choices that may not be optimal from a purely rational standpoint.

Reference Points: The Power of Perspective in Financial Decisions

Our perception of financial outcomes heavily depends on our reference point - typically our current state or expectations. This concept explains why the same objective outcome can be perceived differently by different individuals, or even by the same person under different circumstances.

Let's examine the case of two colleagues, Mark and Sarah, who both received a $5,000 bonus. Mark, who expected a $3,000 bonus, was elated. Sarah, who anticipated $7,000, felt disappointed. Objectively, they received the same amount, but their reference points led to vastly different emotional responses and subsequent financial behaviors.

Mark, viewing his bonus as a gain, became more risk-averse in his investments, wanting to protect his unexpected windfall. Sarah, perceiving her bonus as a loss relative to her expectations, became more risk-seeking, hoping to make up for the perceived shortfall.

The Interplay of Loss Aversion and Reference Points

These two factors - loss aversion and reference points - often interact in complex ways, influencing our financial decisions. Let's look at the story of the Johnson family to see this interplay in action.

The Johnson's had been saving for years to buy their dream home. When they finally accumulated enough for a down payment, housing prices in their desired neighborhood suddenly spiked. Faced with the choice of stretching their budget or looking elsewhere, they opted to take on a larger mortgage than they initially planned.

This decision was driven by both loss aversion and their reference point. The Johnson's reference point was their long-held dream of living in this specific neighborhood. The prospect of "losing" this dream triggered their loss aversion, making them willing to take on additional financial risk to avoid this perceived loss.

While their decision allowed them to achieve their goal, it also placed them under significant financial strain for years to come. This example highlights how the combination of loss aversion and reference points can lead to decisions that may have long-term consequences.

Beyond Rationality: Emotional Factors in Financial Choices

Prospect Theory challenges the notion of humans as purely rational decision-makers, emphasizing the role of emotions and cognitive biases in our choices. This is particularly evident in investment behavior.

Consider the case of Robert, an experienced investor. Despite his knowledge of market cycles, Robert found himself panic-selling stocks during a market downturn. His behavior was driven by loss aversion - the fear of further losses outweighed the potential for future gains.

Conversely, when the market was booming, Robert held onto winning stocks longer than was optimal, a phenomenon known as the disposition effect. His reference point had shifted with each gain, making him reluctant to sell and realize a smaller gain relative to his new expectations.

Robert's experiences demonstrate how even seasoned investors can fall prey to the psychological tendencies described by Prospect Theory. Understanding these tendencies is crucial for making more balanced and rational financial decisions.

Practical Applications: Using Prospect Theory to Improve Financial Decision-Making

While Prospect Theory describes common psychological tendencies, awareness of these patterns can help us make better financial choices. Here's how:

1. Reframe losses as opportunities: Instead of viewing a market downturn as a loss, try to see it as a chance to buy stocks at a discount.

2. Set appropriate reference points: Be mindful of how you set expectations. Unrealistic reference points can lead to perceived losses and risky behavior.

3. Focus on long-term trends: This can help mitigate the impact of short-term losses on decision-making.

4. Use automatic investing: This can help bypass the psychological pain of parting with money regularly.

5. Implement a "cooling off" period: Before making significant financial decisions, especially in response to market changes, give yourself time to overcome initial emotional reactions.

Actionable Tips and Exercises:

1. Loss Aversion Self-Assessment: Write down your reactions to a hypothetical $1,000 gain versus a $1,000 loss. Compare the intensity of your feelings. This can help you understand your degree of loss aversion.

2. Reference Point Identification: List your major financial goals. For each, identify your current reference point. Are these reference points realistic and helpful, or are they setting you up for perceived losses?

3. Decision Journal: For your next few financial decisions, record your thought process, paying attention to how loss aversion and reference points might be influencing you. Review this journal periodically to identify patterns.

4. Reframing Practice: Take a recent financial "loss" and practice reframing it positively. How might this situation present an opportunity or learning experience?

5. Risk Tolerance Experiment: Allocate a small portion of your investment portfolio to a strategy that's slightly outside your comfort zone. Monitor how you feel about this over time to better understand your true risk tolerance.

By engaging with these exercises, you can start to recognize and mitigate the effects of loss aversion and reference dependence in your financial life, potentially leading to more balanced and effective decision-making.

To sum up, Prospect Theory offers profound insights into the psychological factors that drive our financial decisions. By understanding concepts like loss aversion and the impact of reference points, we can become more aware of our own decision-making processes. This awareness, in turn, allows us to make more deliberate and rational choices, potentially leading to better financial outcomes. Remember, the goal isn't to eliminate these psychological tendencies - they're a fundamental part of human nature - but to work with them consciously, using their insights to inform smarter financial strategies.

10.4: Social Comparison Theory and its Role in Financial Satisfaction

Social Comparison Theory, introduced by psychologist Leon Festinger in 1954, posits that individuals assess their social and personal worth by comparing themselves to others. In the realm of personal finance, this theory plays a significant role in shaping our perceptions of financial success and satisfaction. This subchapter explores how social comparisons influence our financial well-being, focusing on two main factors:

1. **Upward Comparisons:** How comparing ourselves to those perceived as better off financially affects our satisfaction and behavior.
2. **Downward Comparisons:** The impact of comparing ourselves to those we perceive as worse off financially.

Let's delve into these factors and examine how they shape our financial perceptions, decisions, and overall satisfaction.

Upward Comparisons: The Double-Edged Sword of Aspiration

Upward comparisons occur when we measure ourselves against those we perceive as more successful or better off financially. These comparisons can serve as motivation for improvement, but they can also lead to feelings of inadequacy and dissatisfaction.

Consider the story of Mike, a mid-level manager at a tech company. Mike was generally content with his salary until he learned that his college roommate, Alex, had just bought a luxury car and a vacation home. Suddenly, Mike's perception of his own financial situation shifted. He began to feel dissatisfied with his income and lifestyle, despite the fact that nothing in his actual financial situation had changed.

Mike's experience illustrates how upward comparisons can negatively impact financial satisfaction. However, upward comparisons aren't always detrimental. For some, they can serve as powerful motivators.

Take the case of Lisa, a small business owner. When she noticed that her competitors were expanding their services and reaching new markets, she felt a mix of envy and inspiration. Instead of letting these feelings discourage her, Lisa used them as motivation to innovate and grow her own business. In this instance, upward comparison served as a catalyst for positive change.

These contrasting examples demonstrate the dual nature of upward comparisons in our financial lives. They can either diminish our satisfaction or drive us to improve our circumstances, depending on how we choose to respond to them.

Downward Comparisons: The Comfort of Relative Advantage

Downward comparisons involve measuring ourselves against those we perceive as less fortunate or successful. These comparisons often serve to boost our self-esteem and increase our sense of financial satisfaction.

Let's examine the case of the Thompson family. The Thompsons lived in a modest home and drove used cars. They occasionally felt dissatisfied with their financial situation, especially when seeing their neighbors' new purchases. However, their perspective shifted dramatically after volunteering at a local homeless shelter.
Seeing the struggles of those less fortunate made the Thompsons realize how much they had to be grateful for. Their house, which had seemed small before, now felt like a blessing. Their used cars, previously a source of embarrassment, became symbols of their financial stability.

This shift in perspective through downward comparison led to a significant increase in the Thompson's financial satisfaction. However, it's important to note that while downward comparisons can increase satisfaction, they can also lead to complacency if not balanced with a drive for personal growth.

The Interplay of Upward and Downward Comparisons

These two types of social comparisons often interact in complex ways, influencing our financial perceptions and behaviors. Let's look at the story of Sarah to see this interplay in action.

Sarah, a freelance graphic designer, frequently found herself caught between upward and downward comparisons. When she landed a big client, she'd compare herself to more established designers, feeling that she still had far to go. This upward comparison motivated her to improve her skills and expand her business.

At the same time, when facing challenges, Sarah would remind herself of struggling artists she knew who couldn't make ends meet. This downward comparison helped her appreciate her progress and maintain her confidence during tough times.

Sarah's ability to balance these comparisons allowed her to stay motivated without becoming overly discouraged or complacent. Her story demonstrates how, when used mindfully, both types of social comparisons can contribute to a healthy financial mindset.

Beyond the Individual: Social Comparison in the Digital Age

The advent of social media has dramatically amplified the effects of social comparison on our financial satisfaction. Platforms like Instagram and LinkedIn provide a constant stream of curated glimpses into others' financial lives, often presenting an unrealistic standard for comparison.

Consider the experience of Tom, a recent college graduate. Scrolling through his social media feeds, Tom saw classmates posting about high-paying jobs, luxury vacations, and new cars. These constant upward comparisons led Tom to feel increasingly dissatisfied with his entry-level position and modest lifestyle.

However, after discussing his feelings with a mentor, Tom realized that social media often presents a skewed reality. He learned to approach these posts with a more critical eye, understanding that they often represent highlight reels rather than everyday realities.

Tom's story underscores the importance of developing a nuanced understanding of social comparisons in the digital age. While social media can exacerbate negative effects of comparison, awareness of this tendency can help us navigate these platforms more mindfully.

Practical Applications: Harnessing Social Comparison for Financial Well-being

Understanding Social Comparison Theory can help us manage its effects on our financial satisfaction. Here are some strategies:

1. Choose comparisons wisely: Focus on comparisons that inspire and motivate rather than those that simply make you feel inadequate.

2. Practice gratitude: Regularly acknowledging what you're grateful for can help balance the effects of upward comparisons.

3. Set personal benchmarks: While it's natural to compare ourselves to others, setting and tracking personal financial goals can provide a more meaningful measure of progress.

4. Limit social media exposure: Be mindful of how social media affects your financial perceptions and limit your use if necessary.

5. Seek diverse perspectives: Expose yourself to a wide range of financial situations to gain a more balanced view of where you stand.

Actionable Tips and Exercises:

1. Comparison Awareness Journal: For one week, note every time you make a financial comparison. Write down who you're comparing yourself to, how it makes you feel, and what you can learn from it.

2. Gratitude Practice: Each day, write down three things you're financially grateful for. This can help balance the effects of upward comparisons.

3. Personal Benchmark Setting: Identify three personal financial goals. Track your progress towards these goals rather than comparing yourself to others.

4. Social Media Audit: Review your social media feeds. Unfollow or mute accounts that consistently make you feel financially inadequate.

5. Diverse Perspective Challenge: Seek out stories of people from various financial backgrounds. This can help broaden your perspective and reduce the impact of narrow social comparisons.
By engaging with these exercises, you can start to harness the positive aspects of social comparison while mitigating its negative effects on your financial satisfaction.

To wrap up, Social Comparison Theory offers valuable insights into how our perceptions of others' financial situations shape our own sense of financial well-being. By understanding the dynamics of upward and downward comparisons, we can develop a more balanced and realistic view of our financial standing. The key is to use social comparisons as tools for motivation and gratitude, rather than sources of anxiety or complacency. With this approach, we can cultivate a healthier relationship with money and a greater sense of financial satisfaction, regardless of how we measure up to others.

10.5: Case Study: Applying These Theories to Real-Life Financial Scenarios

In this subchapter, we'll explore how the theories discussed in previous sections - Prospect Theory and Social Comparison Theory - play out in real-life financial scenarios. By examining these case studies, we'll gain a deeper understanding of how psychological factors influence our financial decisions and satisfaction. We'll focus on two main factors:

1. Decision-making under uncertainty
2. The impact of social comparisons on financial behavior

Let's dive into these case studies and see how these theories manifest in everyday financial situations.

Case Study 1: The Investment Dilemma

Meet Rachel, a 35-year-old marketing executive who recently received a $10,000 bonus. She's considering two investment options:

Option A: A guaranteed 5% return over one year
Option B: A 50% chance of earning a 12% return, but also a 50% chance of losing 2%

Rachel's decision-making process illustrates key aspects of Prospect Theory. Despite the higher potential return of Option B, Rachel chooses Option A. This choice reflects loss aversion - the tendency to prefer avoiding losses over acquiring equivalent gains.

Rachel explains, "I know I could potentially earn more with Option B, but the thought of losing any of my bonus is just too stressful. I'd rather have a sure thing."

This scenario demonstrates how loss aversion can lead individuals to make more conservative financial choices, even when a riskier option might offer a higher expected value.

Transitioning from individual decision-making to social influences, let's examine our next case study.

Case Study 2: The Home buying Pressure

John and Maria, a young couple, are feeling pressured to buy a house. They've been renting comfortably, but recently noticed that many of their friends are becoming homeowners.

Maria explains, "Whenever we see a social media post about a friend's new house, it makes us feel like we're falling behind. Maybe we should stretch our budget and buy now before we miss out."

This situation illustrates Social Comparison Theory in action. John and Maria's satisfaction with their current living situation is diminishing due to upward comparisons with their peers. They're considering making a major financial decision based not on their personal circumstances, but on how they measure up to others.

However, after discussing their situation with a financial advisor, John and Maria decide to wait. They realize that their friends' financial situations might be different from theirs, and that rushing into homeownership could strain their finances.

This case highlights how awareness of social comparison tendencies can lead to more rational financial decisions.

Let's now examine a scenario that combines elements of both theories.

Case Study 3: The Career Crossroads

Alex, a 40-year-old software engineer, is contemplating a career change. He's been offered a position at a startup that comes with a lower base salary but includes stock options. His current job offers stability and a comfortable salary.

Alex's decision-making process involves both Prospect Theory and Social Comparison Theory:

Prospect Theory: Alex is grappling with loss aversion. The potential loss of his stable income looms larger in his mind than the possible gains from the startup's success.

Social Comparison Theory: Alex finds himself comparing his situation to both his current colleagues (downward comparison) and successful startup founders (upward comparison).

Alex reflects, "A part of me wants to play it safe and stay with my current job. I know I'm doing better than many of my college friends. But then I read about these startup success stories, and I wonder if I'm missing out on something big."

After careful consideration, Alex decides to take the startup job. He reframes the situation, viewing it not as a potential loss of stability, but as an investment in his future. He also consciously limits his exposure to startup success stories to avoid unrealistic comparisons.

This case demonstrates how understanding these psychological theories can help individuals make more balanced decisions, taking into account both risk tolerance and personal goals rather than being swayed solely by social pressures or fear of loss.

Practical Applications: Applying Theory to Personal Finance

These case studies illustrate how Prospect Theory and Social Comparison Theory influence our financial decisions. Here are some strategies to apply these insights to your own financial life:

1. Recognize loss aversion: When making financial decisions, ask yourself if fear of loss is disproportionately influencing your choice.

2. Reframe risks as opportunities: Try to view financial risks not just as potential losses, but as potential gains or learning experiences.

3. Be mindful of social comparisons: Recognize when your financial dissatisfaction stems from comparing yourself to others rather than your personal goals.

4. Set personal financial benchmarks: Define success based on your individual circumstances and aspirations, not societal expectations.

5. Seek diverse perspectives: Consult with financial advisors or mentors who can provide objective insights into your financial decisions.

Actionable Tips and Exercises:

1. Decision-Making Diary: Next time you face a significant financial decision, document your thought process. Identify how loss aversion and social comparisons might be influencing you.

2. Social Media Financial Impact Assessment: For one week, note how social media affects your financial satisfaction. Are certain types of posts making you feel inadequate or pressured?

3. Personal Financial Values Clarification: List your top five financial priorities. How do these align with your current behavior? Are any of these priorities influenced more by social pressure than personal desire?

4. Risk Reframing Exercise: Think of a financial risk you've been avoiding. Try to list three potential positive outcomes of taking this risk.

5. Comparison Detox: Challenge yourself to go one month without making financial comparisons to others. Instead, focus on your personal financial progress.

By engaging with these exercises, you can start to apply the insights from Prospect Theory and Social Comparison Theory to your own financial life. Remember, the goal is not to eliminate these psychological tendencies - they're a natural part of how we think - but to become more aware of them so we can make more intentional and personally aligned financial decisions.

To sum up, understanding how Prospect Theory and Social Comparison Theory play out in real-life scenarios can significantly improve our financial decision-making and satisfaction. By recognizing loss aversion, being mindful of social comparisons, and focusing on personal financial goals, we can navigate our financial lives with greater clarity and purpose. These psychological insights, when applied thoughtfully, can lead to more balanced, confident, and personally fulfilling financial choices.

Conclusion

Dear readers, entrepreneurs, and financial explorers,

As we conclude the final chapter of "The Psychology of Money: What is the Connection Between Money and Happiness?", we stand at a crossroads of revelation and opportunity. Our journey through the intricate landscape of financial psychology has illuminated the profound yet often overlooked connection between our wealth and our well-being., we stand at a crossroads of revelation and opportunity. Our journey through the intricate landscape of financial psychology has illuminated the profound yet often overlooked connection between our wealth and our well-being.

To the businesspeople among us: Your acumen in financial matters is undoubtedly sharp, but consider how much sharper it could be when honed by psychological insight. The lessons we've explored – from the quirks of loss aversion to the power of framing – aren't just academic curiosities. They're practical tools that can reshape your decision-making, enhance your leadership, and potentially revolutionize your business strategies.

Entrepreneurs, your path is paved with financial risks and rewards. Armed with the knowledge from this book, you're now equipped to navigate these challenges with a more nuanced understanding. Recognize when fear might be holding you back or when overconfidence might be pushing you towards unwise risks. Let this newfound awareness be your compass in the unpredictable seas of entrepreneurship.

And to every individual seeking to master their personal finances: You now hold the key to unlocking a more fulfilling relationship with money. Whether you're planning for retirement, saving for a dream, or simply trying to find peace in your daily financial life, the insights you've gained can guide you towards decisions that align not just with your bank balance, but with your values and aspirations.

The importance of a balanced and psychologically informed approach to money cannot be overstated. It's the cornerstone of not just financial success, but of a life well-lived. By understanding the psychological forces at play in our financial lives, we can:

1. Make decisions that resonate with our true selves, not just our bank accounts
2. Find contentment in what we have, while still striving for growth
3. Build resilience against the psychological pitfalls that often derail financial plans
4. Improve our relationships by understanding how money impacts our interactions
5. Achieve a sense of financial well-being that goes beyond mere numbers

Now, as we conclude, I extend a call to action to each of you. It is an opportune moment to reassess your relationship with money. I encourage you to:

1. Reflect deeply on your financial beliefs. Are they truly yours, or inherited notions that may no longer serve you?
2. Challenge your assumptions about money and happiness. How might you redefine success in a way that truly resonates with your core values?
3. Implement the practical exercises outlined in this book. Start small, but start today.
4. Engage in open, honest conversations about money with your loved ones, colleagues, and financial advisors.
5. Regularly reassess your financial decisions through the lens of both practical considerations and psychological well-being.

Remember, the goal isn't to amass wealth for its own sake, but to create a financial life that supports your overall happiness and well-being. It's about making money work for you, not the other way around.

As you close this book and step back into your financial life, carry with you the knowledge that you have the power to reshape your relationship with money. You can transcend the anxieties, comparisons, and misconceptions that often cloud our financial judgment. With awareness, intention, and the insights you've gained, you can forge a path to true financial satisfaction and, ultimately, a richer, more fulfilling life.

Thank you for engaging in this journey of exploration alongside me. May your path forward be marked by financial wisdom, psychological balance, and genuine happiness? Here's to your success, not just in your bank account, but in the full, vibrant tapestry of your life.